Galway: politics and

Maynooth Studies in Local History

SERIES EDITOR Raymond Gillespie

This volume is one of six short books published in the Maynooth Studies in Local History series in 2011. Like their predecessors they range widely, both chronologically and geographically, over the local experience in the Irish past. That local experience is presented in the complex and contested social worlds of which it is part. As such they reflect the divide between popular beliefs about women healers in Kildare and the music and dancing in a great house in the same county, the military confrontations of revolutionary Galway and the legal confrontations of breach of promise cases in Limerick and the differing tenant experience of eviction and re-colonisation on the earl of Clanricarde's lands in 19th-century Galway and the colonization of Ráth Cairn with Irish speakers in the 20th century. These local experiences cannot be a simple chronicling of events relating to an area within administrative or geographically determined boundaries since understanding a local world presents much more complex challenges for the historian. It is a reconstruction of the socially diverse worlds of the poor as well as the rich and a consideration of those who took widely contrasting positions on the political issues that preoccupied local communities in Ireland. Reconstructing such diverse local worlds relies on understanding what the people of the different communities that made up the localities of Ireland had in common and what drove them apart. Understanding the assumptions, often unspoken, around which these local societies operated is the key to recreating the world of the Irish past and reconstructing the way in which those who inhabited those worlds lived their daily lives. In addressing these issues, studies such as those presented in these short books, together with their predecessors, are at the forefront of Irish historical research and represent some of the most innovative and exciting work being undertaken in Irish history today. They also provide models which others can follow up and adapt in their own studies of the Irish past. In such ways will we understand better the regional diversity of Ireland and the social and cultural basis for that diversity. If they also convey something of the vibrancy and excitement of the world of Irish local history today they will have achieved at least some of their purpose.

Maynooth Studies in Local History: Number 95

Galway: politics and society, 1910–23

Tomás Kenny

FOUR COURTS PRESS

Set in 10pt on 12pt Bembo by
Carrigboy Typesetting Services for
FOUR COURTS PRESS LTD
7 Malpas Street, Dublin 8, Ireland
www.fourcourtspress.ie
and in North America for
FOUR COURTS PRESS
c/o ISBS, 920 N.E. 58th Avenue, Suite 300, Portland, OR 97213.

ISBN 978-1-84682-293-3

Printed in England
by Antony Rowe Ltd, Chippenham, Wilts.

Contents

Acknowledgments

In the writing of this I have accumulated many debts, with many friends. Laura, Steve, Sarah, Anna, Karen, Danny and especially Aoife have been a brilliant help, often with distraction! Michael and Kelly have provided help and insight to many things within these pages, and I really appreciate all their help through the years. My family have also been terrific, and I thank them sincerely, especially my parents. Indeed, it is to my father that I dedicate this work, as the man who knows more about and has a greater love for all things Galway than anyone I have ever met.

Introduction

The period 1910–23 in Ireland was one of dramatic change; change of governments, of states, of political attitudes and in day-to-day life. This was not something that occurred in isolation, but was rather contextualized within the wider land resettlement that had been accelerating from the first land act of 1870 to the revolutionary years.[1] It is unmatched as a turbulent period in national history, and at a local level in Co. Galway. Despite this there is no local survey of the period. The historiography of Galway is poor, but it is nonetheless surprising that no major survey of the years 1910–23 has been attempted. Local study has been hampered by several factors, perhaps the most pertinent of which was a perception of inaction in the county during the revolutionary years. There is a real need to study local events, for their own merits and to allow the placing of local activity within a national context. John Cunningham's book on 19th century Galway ends at 1914, but in reality is focused on the decades before. The majority of what has been written focuses on the 1916 Rising. As Galway was one of the few areas outside of Dublin to see military action, this is not surprising. There are short articles by Fergus Campbell and Mattie Neilan, and a chapter in Campbell's study of south Galway between 1891 and 1921. This is the sum total of the secondary literature available. The same is true for the War of Independence from 1919 to 1921, on which Campbell's book also contains a chapter, but one which is focused on the agrarian issues of the time. The land issue dominates the diverse strands of these 14 years. It remained unresolved and pervades all aspects of the period.

There have been some pamphlets on specific aspects of the War of Independence, but they are often biased and untrustworthy. The same can be said for the limited literature produced on the Civil War period from 1922 to 1923, which tends to be polemical. Historical research of these years has increasingly concentrated on local studies, but has thus far been confined to the counties which are perceived to have played an important role. Marie Coleman's book on Longford, David Fitzpatrick's work on West Clare, Peter Hart's book on Cork and Michael Farry's book on Sligo are all examples of this. The differences in counties perceived to have been active or dormant can be minor, yet crucial. David Fitzpatrick points to this when he poses the question

Did Longford outdo its neighbours in violence because of the personality of a single blacksmith? If three enterprising brothers had been born a few hundred yards south instead of north of the Clare–Limerick border, would Clare like Connaught have rested in slumber deep throughout the revolutionary years?[2]

Fitzpatrick comes to the conclusion that leadership was of secondary importance, something that as we will see, is not true of Galway.

The national historiography of the conflict has been ever changing, but has improved immeasurably with the opening of the witness statements at the Bureau of Military History in 2003. It has also benefited from peace in Northern Ireland and the increasing distance between the time of writing and the time of study, reducing the bias inherent in much of the earlier work. The next step in the advancement of this historiography is study at a local level. Local initiative drove national events in those years, making such studies tremendously important.

Galway from 1910 to 1923 often seems paradoxical. A highly disruptive county with many of the island's poorest inhabitants, it appeared ready to erupt once politics were radicalized in the absence of emigration during the years of the Great War, 1914–18. Yet revolution as seen in Tipperary, Cork and elsewhere was never to materialize. By any standards of assessment, Galway saw only low intensity fighting throughout the revolutionary years. However, there were a series of events throughout the period in which Galway was catapulted into the national and international limelight. Given that public opinion in Britain and internationally was important in securing British support for a cessation of hostilities, the contribution of Galway, small in many respects, cannot be dismissed from the annals of the War of Independence.[3] The same is true of the Civil War, where isolated events cannot disguise an otherwise quiet conflict, but can inform contemporary popular opinion.

1. Gathering storm clouds, 1910–16

County Galway in 1910 was depressed. The population had fallen from its pre-Famine height of 440,198 in 1841 to just 182,224 six decades later.[1] The haemorrhaging of people was primarily from the countryside, as by the turn of the century the market towns were demographically relatively stable. Emigration was the main reason for continuing depopulation, but the low birth rate was also significant.[2] The excess of births over deaths was only 68 per cent of that found in Mayo, despite Galway having a marginally bigger population and a similar economic structure.[3] There was large-scale discontent over the perceived inequities of the land ownership system. Poverty was rife, and, as relief was doled out in small consistent quantities, families remained on the edge of destitution and without hope of ever breaking the cycle. In fact, the poor law guardians were anxious to avoid any expectation that relief would do anything other than keep people alive, and would certainly not raise living standards.[4] The number of people receiving relief was in significant decline, but this was due to emigration and the perceived stigma attached to it, rather than any improvement in conditions.[5] Private relief was often organized, and individuals such as Alice Stopford Green and Douglas Hyde helped to spearhead a movement aimed at overhauling the entire relief system, which in Connemara they labelled 'a disgrace'.[6] The difference between the west and the east of the county was stark, as the census land valuations dramatically show, with areas like Lettermore, Roundstone and Oughterard worth only a fraction of their east Galway cousins. The drop in population was, not surprisingly, most pronounced in areas like these in Connemara.

Pre-Famine Galway was considered by the authorities to be in a state of 'almost open rebellion' and to a certain degree, little had changed.[7] Following the foundation of the Land League in 1878–9, Galway was the most violent county in the country, and remained one of the most troublesome until the beginning of the 20th-century.[8] The ranch war of 1906–9 was the 'most serious outbreak of agrarian conflict in 20th-century Ireland'.[9] Eleven-month leases on grasslands were highly unpalatable to tenants, leaving landlords in a fraught position. As a result of this continued disaffection, the county was also one of the most highly politicized and radical in Ireland. Galway had the highest ratio of police to people in the entire country.[10] Continuing nervousness about the situation was voiced by the city's Irish Parliamentary Party (IPP) MP, Arthur Lynch, in 1902: 'it would seem that the struggle of Ireland for autonomy may be entering one of those exasperating phases which we have so often seen

before, and that troublesome days are yet on store'.[11] Lynch's defeated opponent
in the 1901 election was a compromise nationalist and unionist candidate –
Horace Plunkett. Badly beaten on polling day, he had some interesting obser-
vations on the influence of the clergy in Galway – '[I] walked through the
Claddagh and was howled at by low fiends of women and children ... certainly
the priest in politics shows at his worst in a place like this. Priests in the polling
booths – priests outside – priests marching their parishoners to the polls like
Salvation Army processions.'[12] These thoughts were echoed by William
O'Malley, another Galway MP – 'any laymen who speaks disrespectfully of
priests, or who opposes them in any way, is strongly suspected of holding
unorthodox views on religion, and he exposes himself to denunciation.'[13]

In general the city did not benefit from the industrial revolution sweeping
Britain. In the mid- and late 19th century many smaller towns were growing,
but Galway city continued its long process of decay.[14] Technically, Galway was
no longer even a city, the corporation having been abolished in 1841.[15] By 1911
the population was only 13,255, a late 19th-century economic surge common
to the other market towns in the county having no effect there. Reminders
of a more prosperous past lingered, as one visitor remarked: 'while there are
quaint structures still to be found in the streets they require looking for and
one must be prepared to endure much squalor and dirt and endless smells.'[16]

Indigenous industry had been dealt a blow with the closure of Persse's
whiskey distillery at Nun's Island in 1908, a major employer which had
supported a large number of subcontractors. There were still several factories
and industries in the city – the Galway Hosiery Factory, the Galway Woollen
Mills, the Bag and Jute Factory and a number of flour mills, all of which used
the fast-flowing river as a source of power and provided local employment,
but they were small and the city was poorly developed industrially. Instead,
many in the city looked to the development of the transatlantic trade as their
ticket to prosperity. The idea was not new – it had been a dream for successive
generations of Galwegians, and at various times looked like it might take off,
particularly after the rail link was established in 1851. A Galway Line to Boston/
Newfoundland had been introduced in 1858 but despite having a transatlantic
mail contract, failed after a few years.[17] The sheltered harbour, plentiful fishing
lanes, and the advantageous geographical position meant there was eternal
optimism for a rebirth of the Line. In the absence of other viable and stable
industry, it dominated the local agenda for almost a century. The optimism was
never justified, and a proposed new port capable of handling substantial
transatlantic trade at Barna was never built. Despite its natural resources, at the
close of the 19th century Galway only had 0.8 per cent of Ireland's seaborne
trade, a percentage that reflected only a fraction of its potential.[18]

Much of the control of industry in the city centred around Máirtín Mór
McDonogh, Galway's most powerful and well-known figure, who was able to
'diversify into almost every sector of the local economy.'[19] His role extended

1 Galway Hosiery Factory, *c*.1910

through business into wider political and social aspects, and he was the Chairman of the Urban District Council, the Employer's Federation and the Harbour Board.[20] He fought against the encroachment of trade unionism, which was slower to start in Galway than elsewhere in the country.[21] Nevertheless it began to gain ground. The Irish Trades Union Congress was held in Galway in 1911, even though the city did not have a trades' council. Increasing labour awareness was emphasized by a speech given by Jim Larkin in the city in June 1911. The following March there was a week-long lockout that ended with substantial concessions to the workers.[22] This was anathema to McDonogh who enlisted the help of employers in the city and employers' federations from England to prevent a repeat. Labour was now well organized however, and in March 1913 over 1,000 workers went on strike for five weeks, attaining minor concessions. The working class were proving to be assertive and providing an impetus for change themselves, much like their rural counterparts.

Along with the Labour movement, the feminist movement was gaining ground in Galway. In 1908 Monica McDonagh became the first woman to be elected as a poor law guardian, in Oughterard. Christabel Pankhurst visited the city in 1911 and gave a well-received speech. Like the holding of the Trades Union Congress in the same year, it proved a springboard for organization, with the establishment of a branch of the Irish Women's Suffrage League some months later.[23] The Urban District Council pledged its support to Women's Suffrage in a motion passed that October. Such gradual changes in Galway life reflected developments in other cities in the United Kingdom, as various marginalized classes fought for recognition.

One major venture of the time was the new newspaper the *Connacht Tribune*, which was launched in 1909 to provide Galway with an 'upright national newspaper, clean and pure in sound, staunch and sound in principle'.[24] The Irish Parliamentary Party MP John Dillon was aware of the importance of the new venture in promoting a nationalist mindset, writing in the paper that 'there was never a time in the history of the national movement when there was so great a field of usefulness for a vigorous and able provincial press.'[25]

Rural Galway was faring even worse than its declining capital, although there was a significant divide between east and west. The west was faced with a far more serious economic situation.[26] The practice of land subdivision was not completely eradicated, and small holdings with poor land left Connemara an extremely difficult place to live in.[27] Land holdings were grossly unequal in the west of Ireland – the 6,000 largest famers held about the same amount of land as the 70,000 smallest.[28] Crop failures had been occurring sporadically since the Famine and remained a constant threat to the populace.[29] The Congested Districts Board (CDB), which is often seen as popular throughout the Western seaboard, was in fact the focus of much disaffection. In early 1910 the Clifden parish priest, Monsignor McAlpine, complained that Connemara was 'shut out' from the CDB – there was no Galway man on the board and he felt the organization was effectively ignoring the county.[30] Slow progress in land distribution and the board's refusal to get involved in relief led to widespread criticism.[31] This grew throughout the year, and in a thinly veiled threat McAlpine told the Connemara executive of the United Irish League (UIL) in June 1911 that people should bring pressure on landlords in order to force the CDB to comply with their demands.[32] The situation was not quite so bad east of the Corrib, where, although land holdings were small, the land was better, and the towns were holding their own.[33]

The entire county was taken under the auspices of the CDB from 1909.[34] While it had local critics, such a development was positive for the county given the large amount of money and effort the CDB put into the areas under their control. Lee and others have been critical of the attempts to foster industry in the rural west by the CDB, suggesting that investment on the east coast would have resulted in a natural migration away from the congested areas rather than emigration.[35] This suggestion has much merit, but equally the lack of a concentrated industrial effort in Galway City resulted in a waste of potential and resources. The city had a rail link, moderate infrastructure and an unparalleled route to the Americas, but the lack of focused investment must be deemed an opportunity missed. There was no migration to speak of within the county in the first decade of the 20th century, despite the city's potential.[36]

David Fitzpatrick has suggested that 'militarism is one of the few Irish stereotypes which evoked almost universal approbation in a bellicose era'.[37]

This seems appropriate when one considers Gilbert Morrissey's view of Galway in the years prior to the Rising: 'in a sense, arms were never put away. If the people were not fighting against the British forces proper, they were making a fair stand against its henchmen, the tyrant landlord class, their agents and bailiffs.'[38] Galway was one of the more lawless parts of the island, due to agrarian agitation and the support agitators received helped to perpetuate the situation. In response to a question about recent activity in Kinvara the Chief Secretary for Ireland, Augustine Birrell, told the House of Commons, 'The police authorities inform me that, in all, nine cattle drives have taken place in the subdistrict of Kinvara. There are four cases of boycotting in the district. The persons concerned, and also one other, are receiving protection.'[39] The County Council were ostensibly unimpressed by any agrarian outrages but the widespread nature of agitation meant that those standing for election had to walk a tightrope when discussing the issue.[40] MPs William O'Malley and James Cosgrave both gave contradictory speeches relating to illegal agrarian action over the years.[41]

Agitation increased through 1910, and was not always aimed at the landlord class. The family home of a prominent United Irish League (UIL) member was shot at in October, while the beginnings of a damaging split in Craughwell between the UIL and local nationalist hardliners led by Tom Kenny could be seen towards the end of the year.[42] Cattle drives continued to be prominent, and arrests were common.[43] Agitation had popular support, as was apparent in Kinvara when over 200 men went to thresh corn in October 1910 to help families who had sons and fathers incarcerated.[44] The levels of support and success made local powerbrokers even more nervous over seemingly constant lawlessness. The bishop of Galway, Dr O'Dea, issued a pastoral letter in early 1912 concerning boycotting and outrages, telling people to 'set their face against evil doers'.[45] Despite the pleas of O'Dea and other clergy, agrarian conflict remained significant in at least 15 counties until 1914.[46] Post-1914 Galway remained consistently violent and agitated.

Politically, the situation within the county was fluid. On the surface the population was staunchly behind the Irish Parliamentary Party (IPP) and the UIL, but people were willing to follow whoever could help solve the land issue. Sinn Féin made some incursions before 1910. In 1907 clubs were set up but most 'ceased to function after a year.'[47] Although small, they had influence, particularly with extreme nationalists and agrarian agitators. Their most important leader was Tom Kenny, a blacksmith from Craughwell who had founded one of the first Sinn Féin clubs in the county in 1907.[48] He was the centre of the county Irish Republican Brotherhood (IRB) as well as its secret society, and favoured radical land redistribution. These new clubs took aim at both the IPP and the UIL. In 1910, when the leaders of the UIL terminated their support for aggressive agitation the organization lost influence to Sinn Féin.[49] While membership of the League had increased, this was largely due to the introduction of the Birrell Land Act and the IPP holding the balance of power after the 1910 elections. Many feared that it was too beholden to larger farmers. One such man was Martin Finnerty from Ballinasloe who that same year formed the United Estates Committee to try and combat the perceived prejudices of the UIL.[50] The new organization followed a militant line, and advocated the use of violence to try and force landlords to redistribute grazing land.[51] The move away from the UIL is reflected in the continued rise of Sinn Féin, who reached the zenith of their pre-Rising power in 1910. Pádraic Ó Máille was due to have run for parliament for Sinn Féin in the January elections of that year, but withdrew at the request of his party. Despite this, local police believed he may have won the seat had he contested it.[52] On an elected political level however, there was unwavering support for the IPP. It enjoyed backing from most of the local newspapers, the UDC, the County Council and the majority of the local clergy.[53]

In 1912 a home rule bill was passed, and the IPP finally appeared within sight of its objective. The House of Lords delayed the implementation of the bill by two years, which allowed Unionists in the north-east of the island time to organize opposition. In 1912 they formed the Ulster Volunteers, and signed the Ulster Covenant in huge numbers. Although such action was a direct threat to the rule of law, its profession of absolute loyalty to London and the Crown meant that it provoked an unsure response from the House of Commons. Due to wavering at Westminster, Unionist forces were allowed to mobilize.[54] This militaristic attitude provoked a similar response from the Nationalist community, who formed the Irish Volunteers. The IRB were heavily involved, but needed a non-physical force man to front the organization. They chose Eoin MacNeill, a respected politically moderate academic. Although he was determined not to be a puppet, the IRB's influence was strong from the outset. MacNeill's influential article, 'The North Began', was published in *An Claidheamh Soluis* in November 1913, the same month as the first meeting of the Volunteers. The movement spread quickly, and the first meeting in Galway took place in the Town Hall on 12 December 1913, with Roger Casement and Eoin MacNeill among the speakers.[55] Six hundred people enrolled after the meeting, but in a pattern repeated throughout the island, few who enrolled on the initial night became active Volunteers.[56] Joining was often spontaneous, and 'with a few exceptions the [new recruits] … had no connection with previous national politics other than through the time honoured medium of the United Irish League.'[57] By October the following year there were 8,381 Volunteers in the county, with comparatively more in east Galway.[58] The IRB's influence in the new organization was pronounced, with Tom Kenny prominent.[59] Similarly, they infiltrated every nationalist organization in the county, such as the Gaelic League and the GAA, often through Galway City solicitor George Nicolls and Tom Kenny.[60]

2 Irish Guards Recruiting Depot, *c.*1914

World War I broke out in July 1914, and its effect was felt immediately – the 'town of Galway went recruiting mad'.[61] Local government was fully behind the war effort – 'to encourage our employees to assist and volunteer in this patriotic work, this council [Urban District Council (UDC)] undertakes to keep open positions for these men who volunteer for service'.[62] The UDC and the County Council both called for an officer training depot and a munitions factory to be placed in Galway throughout the war.[63] This was done ostensibly to show support for the war effort, but the potential for employment and investment was a crucial and persuasive underlying factor. The officer's depot was never established, but an 18-pounder shell factory was, along with others in Dublin, Waterford and Cork. The four employed a very significant 2,148 people, although the factories outside Dublin did not become operational until 1917.[64] Panic and paranoia spread through the county, with any strangers treated with suspicion and often even arrested, the *Galway Express* remarking that 'it is rather unpleasant to be a stranger in Galway at present, especially if your physiognomy presents a cosmopolitan appearance'.[65]

However, support for the war was not unanimous, and in November 1914 there was a split in the Volunteers between those who followed Redmond's policy of supporting the war effort as a means to securing home rule, and those, under MacNeill, who were against enlistment. At the time of the split, there were 9,969 volunteers in 110 companies in Galway, and the majority, as

3 Volunteer Training Camp near Athenry, 1916

elsewhere, followed Redmond. Companies generally went one way or the other as a unit, and dissenting voices could be aggressively silenced. In the relatively loyalist city, the MacNeillite faction collapsed 'after a night of violence that culminated in physical attacks on Volunteers and their homes and businesses'.[66] Those who stayed with MacNeill were most often IRB men, and were more concentrated in the east of the county where land agitation was more-or-less constant and the IRB were stronger.[67]

Despite the support for Redmond, popular opinion soon turned against supplementing the British armed forces, and recruiting declined year on year, finally slowing to a trickle.[68] Fear of conscription grew, and united the community. The Kilkerrin parish priest, Patrick Colgan, reflected the mood of many, telling a large crowd that 'no man from this parish would ever be conscripted to the British Army except over his dead body'.[69] Many clergy began to take an active role recruiting for MacNeill's Irish Volunteers, and their numbers grew.[70] RIC Inspector Rutledge later reflected that the conscription issue had been a turning point – 'I think the rank and file were very much affected by it, the ordinary village boys I think they were very much afraid of being made to join the army'.[71] By April 1916, there were 1,791 Irish Volunteers in the county.[72] Clerical support was ever more prominent, and was crucial to the success of Irish Volunteer recruitment.

The situation in Galway by 1916 was fraught. Nationalist leaders and RIC were unable to halt agrarian violence, and local organizations were ensuring land redistribution was occurring with or without the CDB's assistance. The Volunteer split emphasized the difference between the Nationalist factions in the county, and ensured that a small and well-organized group of radicals were able to provide a strong nucleus for the forthcoming Rising. While this has been studied in great detail and continues to be the subject of much attention, it is often forgotten that by the time of the armistice in November 1918 at least 1,107 Galway men had fought in the Great War, of whom an estimated 755 died.[73]

2. The Rising and its aftermath, 1916–18

Prior to the Easter Rising the situation in Galway continued to be troubled. The Great War had shut the traditional valve of emigration: in 1914 2,181 people emigrated from the county, but that figure was reduced to 1,016 from 1915 to 1918.[1] Additionally the work of the CDB was virtually halted during the 1914–18 period.[2] There was criticism of it as class based, which was substantiated to a degree when they allowed graziers to let acquired land waiting to be redistributed.[3] Agitation and intimidation of graziers continued apace, with the RIC acknowledging that these tactics continued to be successful. Indeed, William O'Malley MP admitted that breaking the law was the only resort for some.[4]

Recruiting for the British Army had almost totally dried up. A clock with the number of recruits was to be placed in Eyre Square, and recruiting posters went up in increased volume in an effort to improve recruiting, particularly in the supposedly loyal city.[5] Letters were sent to what were considered likely recruits in 1915 as the authorities became desperate – 'only 45 recruits have joined the army since June. 2,900 must be obtained by October'.[6] Such measures met with no success, as the appetite for being a part of the War had vanished.[7] The situation was mirrored throughout Connacht, a region the authorities looked at with disdain, describing its levels of recruitment as 'miserable, absolutely miserable'.[8]

In the midst of these deepening social problems Liam Mellows was sent to Galway in early 1915 to organize the Irish Volunteers.[9] An English-born republican, his arrival was to change forever nationalist politics in Galway. Based in Athenry he was initially treated suspiciously by some of the nationalist leaders in the east of the county, notably Tom Kenny and Larry Lardner. Lardner was captain of the Galway brigade and as we have seen, Kenny's influence was widespread, so great in fact that the Chief Secretary was reputed to ask 'Was Ireland to be governed by a water bailiff in Dublin [John MacBride] and a blacksmith in Galway [Tom Kenny]?'[10] He was the face of the more radical body politic in Galway. While an avowed nationalist looking for political freedom, Kenny wanted economic freedom through land redistribution and was prepared to fight to get it. The arrival of a young Mellows from Dublin undermined Kenny and Lardner and created tension in the leadership.[11]

Despite Kenny's and Lardner's aversion, Mellows blended in well, and became popular, particularly with ordinary Volunteers, as in the case of Proinsias

4 Galway City Corps, 1916

Ó hEidhin: 'I thought when I first met him that he was only a delicate little chap who was very enthusiastic about the movement and who might be able to give a very fine lecture on patriotism or even how to fight, but no more. I very soon found out my mistake.'[12] Fr Thomas Fahy, who would go on to be chaplain to the Volunteers in the Rising, recalled after meeting him in 1915 that he was 'astonished by the impressive way that he assured me of their determination to fight'.[13] Mellows began a period of intense reorganization 'in the localities which had always been disaffected on account of agrarian agitation. He rallied to his standard all young men who were members of secret societies, with pronounced disloyal feelings.'[14] Shortly after his arrival Galway was divided into four brigades: Galway, Athenry, Gort and Loughrea, which reflected the geographical bias towards the east of the county in which the Volunteers were stronger.[15] Mellows was arrested twice – in July 1915 and in March 1916, and spent months in England under house arrest.[16] The increasing strength and hostility of the Volunteers was demonstrated on St Patrick's Day 1916 when a parade of MacNeill's Volunteers took place in the city. Between 600 and 1,000 took part, with about 200 armed.

Early in 1916, while Mellows was in England, Pádraic Pearse visited Athenry to discuss plans for a Rising.[17] He wanted men to hold the River Suck on the eastern border of the county while taking Galway City and, if possible, to then march on Dublin.[18] While Lardner told Pearse that they could do so, he was shouted down by more reasonable voices.[19] The plan was then modified to having the Western Volunteers holding the line of the Shannon, with the help

5 Workers at Galway National Shell Factory, 1917

of their Ulster counterparts who were to join up with them.[20] However, this would have necessitated marching long distances, most of it through territory occupied by militant Unionists. This was impractical, and so again the plan was rearranged, with more modest objectives; to hold as much of the county as was possible, await word from elsewhere in the country, and take it from there. From an over-complicated plan, they arrived at an over-simplified one, one without clearly defined objectives – a flaw which was to lead to indecision and inaction in Easter week. Despite the best-laid plans, in Galway as elsewhere the Rising was to be undermined by two crucial events – the capture of the *Aud* on 20 April and MacNeill's countermanding order to stop the Rising in Dublin. The arms from the expected arrival of the *Aud* were to be sorted in Abbeyfeale, and a quantity of them sent on to Gort for the Galway Volunteers.[21] The seriousness of these events was acknowledged by the RIC Inspector General, who said afterward the relative failure of the Rising 'must be ascribed to the fortunate arrest of Sir R.Casement and the failure of the German ship to land the required arms and ammunition. There is no reason to believe that if these arrangements had not miscarried the Irish Volunteers in any county would have held back. In fact the evidence is all the other way.'[22]

Before the Rising many of the leaders at a local level knew of impending action, but were not informed of a date. The secrecy led to confusion and misinformation. A few days before Easter Tom Kenny assured IRB men in Craughwell that there were no immediate plans for insurrection.[23] Communication was so confused that John Hosty went to Dublin to try and determine some sort of continuity in orders after a high-level meeting between himself, George Nicolls, Liam Lardner, Michaél Ó Droighneáin and Patrick Callanan.[24] By the time he arrived back, others had heard the news, and had received Pearse's order and MacNeill's countermanding order.

On Easter Monday Volunteers assembled under Mellows' command at Kileeneen, in the east of the county. Their numbers were not initially large due to continuing poor communication, with Pádraig Thornton, captain of the Moycullen Company and Ó Droighneáin, head of the Spiddal brigade, among others, receiving conflicting messages.[25] Ó Droighneáin went into Galway in search of news, but was arrested there, as was George Nicolls, one of the most important leaders in the city, and John Faller, who helped fund the Volunteers.[26]

John D. Costello in North Galway recalled that they were to have heard from Athenry a few days prior to the Rising but no word ever came, and thus 'the failure of our not taking part with Mellows was entirely the fault of the Athenry IRB.'[27] In the city 'the uncertainty of the Rising coming off left the Volunteers without an opportunity of arranging to link up with county units.'[28] The Kinvara company 'knew nothing of the … Rising' until the Wednesday, and although they mobilized that evening they never met up with the main force of Volunteers, another missed opportunity all the more pertinent as they were almost as well armed as the main body of Volunteers.[29] Poor communication thus doomed the Rising in Galway before it began, with many companies who wished to be out unable to participate. That is not to suggest that the mobilization of small companies would have significantly altered the ultimate course of events, but it would undoubtedly have complicated what turned out to be a simple enough quandary.

Those who were at Kileeneen were devoid of real ideas and this was emphasized when the party attempted to intercept an RIC convoy that had captured local leader Pádraic Ó Fathaigh in Gort. It was assumed he was being taken to Galway City jail when, in fact, he was being brought in the opposite direction to Limerick. Four RIC men on a reconnaissance mission were captured at the barricade though. Mellows instead turned his attention to Clarenbridge barracks, which had seven RIC men, and was not thought to be a difficult target. There was a stand-off that included the local parish priest, Fr Tully, pleading with the Volunteers to back down. Mellows refused, but soon realized the futility of his attack, and moved towards Athenry, travelling towards the strategic barracks of Oranmore, gathering numbers as they went. On the road, they met Joe Howley, the local captain, who had attempted an attack in Oranmore. Police arrived from the city as Volunteers were attaching explosives to Oranmore bridge. An engagement followed in which several RIC men and one Volunteer were wounded. The Volunteers successfully withdrew, and were followed by the RIC, who then stripped the barracks of arms and returned to Galway. They then retreated towards Athenry, Mellows met Lardner who informed him that the RIC were surrounded in Athenry, but were too strongly armed to attack, as the 700 or so rebels had only 30 shotguns and 200 rifles.[30] Similarly, the RIC concentrated themselves in the larger towns while they awaited reinforcements. During this time, the rebels had virtually complete control of the countryside, which should have allowed for the leadership to be well informed. Instead 'a large number of false reports were being sent out to Mellows at Moyode', and news from Dublin was sporadic and incomplete.[31]

One hundred British reinforcements arrived into the City port on three ships on Thursday 27 April. These were two sloops, HMS *Snowdrop* and HMS *Laburnum*, and a cruiser, HMS *Birmingham*, which began to shell the position the rebels had taken up in the model farm outside of Athenry.[32] Although a contemporary newspaper account declared that the naval vessels had compelled 'them to retire to Moyode Castle at Athenry', in reality there was little chance of them being successful.[33] In fact, it has been argued that the only reason the Royal Navy pursued such a course was to encourage the loyalists, and discourage the rebels.[34] After another brief encounter with a small band of RIC men the Volunteers realized their defensive position was poor and retreated to Moyode Castle just outside Athenry.

There, very little happened, despite Kenny trying to pursue a more radical direction by raiding nearby grazier farms for cattle. He was firmly blocked by Mellows, leading to a lasting bitterness between them, and all they raided for was food, commandeering two cartloads of flour meant for a Loughrea bakery.[35] The insurgents' activities petered out. Fr Thomas Fahy recalled that Mellows initially refused to disband the Volunteers – 'he would fight it out to the end. These men had joined him voluntarily and he would never ask them to go away'.[36] However, on Friday evening the party marched to Limepark, where, after consultation with officers and company captains, he bowed to the inevitable and disbanded his men. Fr Fahy addressed the Volunteers, and emphasized the hopelessness of their situation, telling them 'that the sacrifice contemplated would be useless, that the position we were in was untenable, resistance futile and that we had nothing to offer in the nature of retaliation, and that for future service to our country as living Volunteers, we would be more useful than to go through the Holocaust that would be inevitable.'[37] Mellows had waited as long as he could in the vain hope that Clare and Limerick would rise up and aid them. Michael Brennan, who later became one of the most prominent republican leaders in the War of Independence, had on Wednesday of Easter week tried to come to Galway with men, but 'was met and turned back on every road by RIC patrols'.[38] The lack of support from the neighbouring counties was a bitter blow to Mellows.[39]

After the rising Kenny went on the run to Boston, not returning until 1923. Given the paucity of leaders in the War of Independence the absence of Kenny for those years was a blow to any hope of large-scale guerrilla activity in

Galway, particularly given his profound influence in Craughwell. The other leaders also went on the run, while ordinary Volunteers went home only to be picked up by the RIC the following week.

The public in Galway were ill informed throughout the Rising, and were hungry for information, 'The fact that there was positively no definite information to go on gave scope for wildest individual conjecture as to the nature and magnitude of the events'.[40] Scared of what lay outside the city, the public helped set up a militia, and a curfew was enacted for the week. RIC retreated to the city from the county, leading to a siege mentality throughout the Rising. Unsurprisingly therefore, the reaction was similar to elsewhere, damning at first, with the *Connacht Tribune* declaring scathingly that there were three types of nationalists – impractical separatists, deluded Germanophiles and realistic Home Rulers.[41] Volunteers were attacked as they were marched through the city.[42] The local authorities' response was predictably aggressive, as the councils were concerned about the situation getting out of hand and radicals gaining support. The County Council unanimously passed a resolution condemning the Rising.[43] At a meeting of the Urban Council Máirtín Mór McDonogh condemned the Rising but appealed for clemency for all but the ringleaders.[44]

The executions are often too simplistically given as the reason for the nations shift towards sympathy for the rebels, but there is no doubt that they played a crucial role. From a loyalist family in the city, Frances Moffett recounted the horror of the paper arriving every day with news of the leader's deaths, culminating in the news of Connolly's execution, which was 'generally considered impossible.'[45] Requiem Mass was held in the Augustinian Church in the City in July 1916 for the repose of the souls of those who died in the Rising. There was a prominent attendance of clergy, and the presiding priest, Fr Travers OSA, declared that they were honouring those who died 'in the recent rebellion, who died as Irishmen and Catholics and who knew how to die.'[46] Although a small gesture, it showed opinion was beginning to shift perceptibly away from the IPP towards Sinn Féin, something recognized by both councils, who appealed in August for the release of both political and agrarian prisoners held without charge.[47]

And yet, were it not for the capture of the *Aud* there is every likelihood that the Rising would have had far greater success in Galway. A large portion of the ships arms were destined for the west, which would have turned the rebels into a more formidable and confident group. Certainly this feeling was echoed by County Inspector Rutledge, head of the west Galway constabulary who declared that had the rebellion occurred without confusion, order and counter-order it 'would have embraced the whole County and we could not have held it.'[48] This did not come to pass, and the RIC and British army were well informed, and able to get their house in order after being surprised by the rebels. Without greater arms and men Mellows band had no ability to achieve either military victory or the notoriety that Pearse attained in Dublin. Although the Rising is often thought of as 'a glorious failure', the fact that the rebels had plans to march on Dublin were everything to go well enough initially in the county was testament that failure was not the only possible result – blood sacrifice did not have the same resonance for Mellows in Galway as it did for Pearse in Dublin. Had the *Aud's* cargo arrived, the potential for a sustained effort against British authority in the area would have been there – 3,000 rifles were earmarked for Galway.

Mellows had control of much of the countryside for days, and a large band of men with him, and yet all that came of it militarily was ill-thought-out skirmishes and abortive raids on barracks. Poorly equipped and armed with a plan, which had evolved several times to the point of confusion, the rebels did little rebelling, instead hiding out at various locations. The Galway Rising suffered from lack of arms and the countermanding order, but also, crucially, from a lack of direction and ambition.

The Galway Volunteers had, in the main, not benefited from the land acts which are too often seen by historians as having solved the land question.[49] Fitzpatrick has written that 'Ireland in 1913 was a country in which a remarkably large part of the people was apparently satisfied with its lot.'[50] For Mellows and the wider Volunteer leadership, the Rising was a fight against imperial rule, but for many of the ordinary Volunteers it was a means to securing land they felt was rightfully theirs – the latest chapter in land agitation and violence in Galway as well as an ideological attack on British rule. Nonetheless, a sizeable force assembled and was ready to fight on Easter Monday, and compared with activities in the rest of the country, militant republicanism appeared to be in good health in Galway.

Large numbers of men were arrested the week after the Rising and sent on to prisons in Britain, the most famous of which was Frongoch, in North Wales. 322 men from Galway were sent there, out of a total of 1,804.[51] This amounts to 17.85 per cent. However, of the 30 inmates who later became TDs, only 2, or 6.66 per cent were from Galway.[52] The reputation of Frongoch as a university from which many of the main players of the War of Independence graduated is warranted generally, but not so much in Galway's case.

Gilbert Morrissey described the effect the arrests had on the economy, as many of the men arrested were 'the bread winners for their families and when they were imprisoned after the Rising, the families suffered. The neighbours at that time were not as sympathetic as they became as the fight progressed, and there were no funds out of which any provision could be made towards the amelioration of their conditions.'[53] He continued, 'Many of the interned Volunteers belonged to the farming class. At that time, they were not as well-off as they became two or three years later. They could not afford to pay hired men and their crops were left unattended until the general release in December 1916.'[54]

The majority were released in time for Christmas, and public opinion was now firmly in their favour. George Nicolls returned to a rapturous welcome in Galway City in a scene that was replicated throughout the county and the country.[55] By August 1917 the County Council had sensed this change of mood and attempted to rescind its earlier resolution condemning the Rising. Even though it did not pass (the vote was 11–11), it was important considering the make-up of the council had not changed since the Rising.[56]

Grassroots support for Sinn Féin was tested in the 1918 elections, and they won all five seats in Galway. Out of 40,496 votes cast in Galway, 31,271 or 77.22 per cent were cast for Sinn Féin.[57] That support was consistently strong in each of the constituencies, with a 77.15 per cent share in Connemara, 68.99 per cent in North Galway and 85.90 per cent in South Galway. Liam Mellows was returned unopposed in East Galway; had there been an election there, it would undoubtedly have increased Sinn Féin's share of the vote. The Galway elections are interesting in a national context. Countrywide, Sinn Féin achieved 46.9 per cent of the vote, which would have been higher but for 25 of its candidates being returned unopposed. The support for Sinn Féin was higher in Galway specifically, and the West in general, than elsewhere in the country.[58] It was not the result of an entirely free and fair election, with both sides willing to influence people's votes – 'Volunteers did [their] duty at the polling booths on polling day.'[59] However Sinn Féin was undoubtedly the most popular political movement in Galway.

Although Galway had huge grassroots support for Sinn Féin, the geography of that movement 'was quite distinct from that of the IRA.'[60] This distinction meant that the large-scale Sinn Féin presence in Galway did not necessarily mean that there was a significant militant presence ready to fight in the forthcoming War of Independence. Sinn Féin, while separate from the Volunteers/IRA, had nonetheless implicitly endorsed military means for achieving their objectives in their 1918 manifesto. One could be forgiven for thinking the stage was set for large-scale operations in Galway during the subsequent war. However, that never materialized. Rather there was large-scale discontent, seen through continual agrarian agitation, which remained a feature after the armistice and into 1919.[61]

3. The War of Independence, 1919–21

The War of Independence began on 21 January 1919 with the meeting of the first Dáil and an ambush at Soloheadbeg in Tipperary, yet some of its most prominent features were in evidence earlier in Galway. Local RIC were being boycotted in 1917, and a Sinn Féin arbitrary court sat as early as 13 January 1918.[1] A bridewell was set up, and was in use in Killeeneen Hall in March 1918.[2] Yet, despite this, the early period of the War in Galway was notable for the lack of any real activity. Support for Sinn Féin and the separatist movement, already channelled through the ballot box, was strong politically and also with the younger clergy. Addressing a large meeting in early 1919, George Nicolls, Fr O'Meehan and Fr Grogan, veterans of the Rising, emphasized that they wanted nothing less than 'their full right of Irish Independence.'[3]

Prior to the Soloheadbeg ambush there were plans to take advantage of Britain's continued participation in the First World War, and while they did not succeed, they are proof of the ambitious thinking of the Volunteers. In spring 1918 Mícheál Ó Droighneáin went to Dublin to meet Michael Collins and discuss plans to land arms from a German submarine in Galway in May of that year.[4] The landing never materialized, because, according to Ó Droighneáin, the submarine was captured in the North Sea, but not before the arms were sent to the bottom. The news did not reach all expectant Volunteers however, as Ó Droighneáin had to turn away Limerick Volunteers who had come to claim their share.

The period leading to the Armistice in November 1918 was characterized politically by RIC clampdowns on many prominent Sinn Féiners, and the constant disruption of recruiting meetings in the city by the Irish Volunteers – including one occasion in 1918 where they barricaded a large crowd in the Town Hall. They cut the electrical wires and released 'test tubes filled with foul smelling liquid.'[5] For the wider society, the arrival of the deadly Spanish flu in spring 1918 was a more pressing issue. In North Galway an average of 10 people a week died.[6] The flu's victims were predominately healthy young adults, which tended to demoralize communities and their ability to function. The pandemic alienated the public from the British, despite it being a global pandemic, as it was held as another example of the failure of the State to protect its citizens.

Scattered RIC raids and arrests aside, 1919 was uneventful. The Volunteers were busy organizing, drilling and raiding for arms.[7] There were some agrarian incidents, but they were relatively isolated, such as the shooting in April of Florimund Quinn, a local magistrate and farmer over a land dispute.[8] While some reaped the benefits of a virtual monopoly on agricultural trade with Britain, for many the economic situation remained serious. At W.T. Cosgrave's suggestion, a fund was opened for the fishermen of the island of Gorumna just off Galway, who were in extreme poverty.[9] The fund attracted significant media coverage, and it is possible that Galway's most useful national contribution to republicanism was to continue as the face of both Old Ireland and of poor and failed British governance.

The first recognized act which could be attributed to the conflict is an isolated attack on Derrybrien Barracks in August 1919.[10] Like so many Volunteer attacks, it was unsuccessful, but forced the local RIC to withdraw. In January 1920 a new phase of the conflict began as IRA GHQ officially sanctioned attacks on RIC barracks.[11] Craughwell barracks was to be attacked, but the Athenry Company needed support from the wider Galway leadership, in arms, expertise, and manpower. Despite a well-conceived plan, Gilbert Morrissey received very little support from the Galway Brigade.[12] It resulted in the attack being called off, and Brigade headquarters never contacted Morrissey to enquire as to why this was the case.[13] Such poor leadership was not uncommon and left individual companies isolated and short of morale. Nonetheless Roundstone and Castlehackett barracks were attacked on 6 and 9 January respectively, followed by several similar actions throughout the year on various barracks that had not yet been evacuated by the RIC.[14] These attacks were rarely successful, but forced the RIC into retreating from their isolated barracks. Those abandoned were burned, including five in April, as part of a coordinated national attack in memory of the Easter Rising four years previously.[15] Galway became steadily more violent throughout the year, but much of the violence took the form of agrarian rather than political agitation and the events of early 1920 continued in that tradition.[16] Cathal Brugha had been worried in 1917 that radical elements of Sinn Féin in the west were merely channelling that party as a vehicle to accelerate land reform.[17] He was right to be concerned, as that was exactly what was occurring – 'to have Sinn Féin membership was apparently advantageous when it came to allocating the commandeered land.'[18] Although the Nationalist leadership was aware of the problem, they could do little to stop it.

In 1920 Captain H.B.C. Pollard wrote of land redistribution by force that Irishmen 'deplore the method, but condone or even uphold the motive.'[19] Agrarian action was popular because it was successful, and in the face of an impotent government and a nationalist community that needed small farmer's support, it only became more successful. In Spring 1920 what Kevin O'Shiel called 'The last land war' began in Galway, spreading quickly across Connacht, and to a degree elsewhere although 'in Ulster and Leinster, trade unions gave it a more organized form'.[20] The CDB's ability to transfer land to small farmers on uneconomic holdings had been severely curtailed during the war, leading to discontent among the small farming classes who were without the traditional emigration outlet. The Board's failure to achieve 'the destruction of the large-scale ranching system' and their apparent collusion with it, had adversely affected their chances of influencing the local community.[21] When the RIC vacated barracks throughout the county, an already lawless society gained even more freedom. It is unsurprising such a course of action occurred – land issues were never far from the surface in Galway. This type of action had previously been implicitly supported by the official organ of Sinn Féin in the county, the *Galway Express*, in which local branches placed notices suggesting that if necessary they would seize land from graziers.[22] Patrick Treacy, a Volunteer from Kiltullagh, admitted cattle driving and land agitation, but claimed it was part of a plan to bring the RIC out into the open.[23] While this may possibly have been true in the isolation of Treacy's case, the wider agitation was taking advantage of the RIC's absence and not trying to goad them into open engagements.

In Oughterard and Headford in April 1920 there was forcible agitation for redistribution, and the County Inspector for East Galway noted that the 'hungering for land' was prevalent everywhere, and getting out of hand.[24] Cattle driving and intense intimidation were the norm.[25] Landlords were threatened by large crowds, and these threats were taken all the more seriously after the murder of Frank Shawe-Taylor in March.[26] He had grazed about 1,000 acres near Athenry and had refused to give up his land for some time. His death focussed the minds of many of his peers, and they ironically turned to Dáil Éireann for support. The Sinn Féin leaders could not allow a political struggle to turn into a land-based conflict, as it would erode support both at home and abroad for any prospective new state. It would also distract from their more immediate problem of fighting a war against British forces. A series of three Land Conferences were held nationally in May 1920, one of which took place in Galway. Sinn Féin laid out their agrarian policy in an effort to both reassure and mollify locals.[27] Many clergy also came out against forcible land grabbing, including Thomas O'Doherty, the bishop of Clonfert, who forcefully condemned locals for their actions, which brought shame on Sinn Féin.[28]

Nonetheless, it remained a feature of life in Galway until the truce.[29] As the *Connacht Tribune* reported – 'no land act was ever capable of making the radical change in outlook in so short a space of time that this movement has already done.'[30] Despite the best efforts of local and national leaders, there was no real incentive for local people to limit their agitation, as it had yielded results, and continued to do so. Intimidations, shootings and cattle driving were persistent, although they were to take a back seat to a more ideologically driven republicanism for the remainder of the conflict.

Reorganizing the Volunteers in the region was a priority. In the aftermath of the Rising, many of the leaders had left – Kenny remained in Boston until

1923, and Mellows, although TD for Galway, was no longer based in the county. In the absence of these top men, the leaders in individual areas were often not up to the challenges. Their appointment of leaders had often been 'of an honourary nature and had nothing to do with their qualification from a military point of view'.[31] Dublin was aware of this, and was anxious to spread the fight from the south and south west of the country. The brigades were all reorganized in 1920 and the new structure invigorated the Volunteers. Richard Mulcahy offered money and men to the West Connemara brigade, and better direction began to be given from above.[32]

Two Volunteers from Oranmore, John Furey and Michael Joyce, went on hunger strike for 10 days in April and May 1920 in a successful effort to receive political status. A large crowd gathered outside Galway Jail to support the men.[33] The level of support worried the authorities, particularly as Galway was believed to be one of the most loyal towns in Ireland only a short time before.[34] Support for the Volunteers was strong countywide – 'the local people did everything in their power towards our maintenance and comfort on all occasions. Their circumstances had vastly improved from those of a few years earlier owing to high prices obtained for their produce following World War I. I think the economic circumstances had a very great bearing on the outcome of the War of Independence'.[35] The agitated citizens vented their anger at the government through support for the rebels and a more coherent labour movement, with a union broadsheet declaring 'well the Worker's council is formed in Galway, and it's here to stay ... for the good and welfare of the whole community and not for the profits of a few bloated parasites. Up Galway!'[36]

The Black and Tans (na Dúchrónaigh) arrived in spring 1920, adding extra troops to the already heavily garrisoned city.[37] Temporary constables established to target the IRA, they quickly earned a bad reputation for their attacks and attitudes to the civilian population – 'leading citizens had sent their wives and children away as bombing shops and houses were part of the Black and Tans' evening entertainment on pay nights.'[38] The County Council proposed in June 'that we ... hereby enter our emphatic protest against the treatment of political prisoners in Galway jail. From information in hand, we are aware that Messrs. Hoey, Staunton, Doherty and Jordan were deprived of their clothes and bed boards, and manacled and kicked in their cells.'[39]

When four RIC men were ambushed at Aughle, near Tuam, with two fatalities, the Black and Tans responded by sacking Tuam on the night of 19 July, the first such reprisal in the country. The devastation was immense, estimated at £100,000.[40] The attack followed a deliberately conceived plan, aimed at buildings associated with republicanism. The Town Hall was destroyed, less than a week after the first public district Sinn Féin court was held there, while several large businesses in the town met a similar fate.[41] Archbishop Gilmartin of Tuam was outraged, and claimed that 'the District Inspector did not attempt to justify the wreckage, but said that it was police who were from

Galway who were principally responsible for it.'[42] The increasingly fractured nature of events was straining the power structure within the British forces, and the more militant Black and Tans and Auxiliaries were willing to go further than the regular RIC and British Army.

Indeed, some had ill conceived ideas of the strength of the IRA in Galway – on being posted to the west of the county, a new Black and Tan was nervous of what he might find – 'Connemara was reported to be the storm centre of all the trouble'.[43] This was not the case and Michael Brennan, head of the IRA in East Clare, was asked for assistance to help kick start the war in Galway– 'a number of Galway men (particularly Laurence Kelly of Loughrea and Jim Reilly from near Portumna) had come to me in Clare on several occasions with appeals to bring the column to Galway. They said the Volunteer organization had collapsed there and a show of armed force would be a magnificent organizing agency'.[44]

Galway, as capital of Connacht, often held prisoners from outside the county, such as Ned Lyons, Commandant of Newport Battalion. He was moved to Galway jail and tortured. His brother recalled how Lyons went missing after the truce and was finally found by his family in Dundrum insane asylum, before dying there in 1924.[45] Word of atrocities such as these became public, and along with reprisals these further isolated the already beleaguered British Forces – the District Inspector for West Galway at the time decried the ever increasing hostility against his charges; they 'have to take the necessities of life by force. Their lives are miserable and their children suffer in the schools and nobody cares.'[46] Unsurprisingly, many RIC men began to resign, some harassed by local Volunteers, some sick of the isolation, and others ideologically opposed to the direction the conflict was taking with the Black and Tans. The *Connacht Tribune* in September alone lists 14 men who had resigned in the previous week.[47] The Black and Tans themselves were low on morale, and some were sympathetic to the Volunteers cause: 'they, at least, conceived themselves to be fighting for a just cause, whereas we knew that we were not, and that we were merely the catspaws of a political junta in London.'[48]

Similarly, local government was under severe pressure, although that pressure came from the British Forces. The local elections in 1920 had seen a strong Sinn Féin majority take over the Urban District Council, while the County Council saw a clean sweep of Sinn Féin candidates.[49] Now openly pro-Dáil Éireann, both local government councils rescinded their predecessors' resolutions condemning the Rising.[50] The County Council announced they would pay IRA police out of funds previously used to pay enemy forces, and their public statements were ever more aggressive.[51] Accordingly they found themselves targets, and Councillor Michael Walsh, of the Urban District Council, was murdered on 19 October 1920 by five disguised men who claimed to be secret police, but whom the local IRA believed to be a Black and Tan named Miller.[52]

6 Funerals of Seán Mulvoy and Seamus Quirke, 1920

7 Seán Mulvoy and Seamus Quirke

As the year went on the *Galway Observer* and the *Connacht Tribune*, both constitutional nationalist papers, drifted towards republicanism. The Irish railway strike in November meant none of the daily national papers arrived until the evening. In response the *Connacht Tribune* printed a daily paper to try and keep the locals up to date, and it adopted a more aggressive tone towards the British Forces. Matters in Galway came to a head in November 1920, when the eyes of the entire conflict briefly turned towards the west. Ellen Quinn was killed in Kiltartan near Gort on 1 November. Unarmed, heavily pregnant, and with a young child in her arms, her killing caused consternation both in Ireland, and in Britain, where the Chief Secretary endured questioning over the event in the Commons.[53]

At the railway station in the city, a gun battle on 8 September 1920 led to the deaths of three people, Edward Krumm, a Black and Tan, and two Volunteers, Seamus Quirke and Sean Mulvoy. The town was placed under curfew two days later, and the funerals were the biggest the city had seen, although they would be surpassed in a matter of weeks.[54] Over 40 clergy of various ranks presided over the Mass. The shootings led to a reprisal in the city on 21 November, in which the *Galway Express*, the Sinn Féin Hall and several private houses were burned down. The muffling of the Sinn Féin mouthpiece increased the speed at which the other local papers moved towards supporting the rebels. They had to do so carefully however, lest the same fate befall them.

The next major event began with an execution by the IRA of a local informer, Patrick Joyce, the principal of Barna National School. Volunteer Joe Togher worked in the Post Office, and in intercepting letters to the British Army and RIC, discovered Joyce was passing on information about the Volunteers in Connemara, including their movements, and the names of all the Brigade Commandants. He sent the evidence to Brigade Commandant Mícheál Ó Droighneáin from Connemara.[55] They determined Joyce was the informant from his handwriting, and after getting approval from Dublin he was subsequently court-martialled and executed on 15 October.[56] As Joyce was a devout Catholic the IRA let it be known that a priest had been with him at the time of his death.[57] They had brought in Fr O'Meehan from near Headford to perform this function, but it was widely assumed it was Fr Michael Griffin, a young priest in the city with known republican sympathies and towards whom Patrick Joyce had been antagonistic.[58] Fr Griffin was arrested on 14 November at his house in the city, after being enticed outside by a man local Volunteers were convinced was William Joyce, later the infamous Lord Haw Haw.[59] Joyce had the timing of the truce to thank for his life, 'I [Joe Togher] intercepted a letter from Joyce to an Auxie, which, after being broken down, revealed that Joyce had the RIC cipher which was in use that particular month … had we received this information earlier, Joyce would have been executed.' Fr Griffin's body was found in a bog in Barna a week later. Prior to the finding of the body, David Lloyd George had insisted in the

8 Group of Black & Tans, 1920

Commons that no Crown forces were involved in his disappearance, a statement which had no credibility once Griffin's remains were found.[60] The local IRA conducted an investigation on the orders of Michael Collins, and decided an Auxiliary named Nichols was responsible.[61]

Britain was already demonstrably losing the propaganda war against the IRA, and such incidents further increased pressure on the government, both at home, in Ireland, and abroad. Locally, the events from his disappearance to the discovery of his body led to widespread 'anguish and anxiety.'[62] Griffin's funeral was a huge affair, with an estimated 12,000 attending – a remarkable figure given that only 14,000 lived in the city at the time.[63] The Black and Tans made a concerted effort to dissuade people from attending, as the photographic evidence dramatically shows, but sheer weight of numbers made the crowd impossible to police, and turned the event into a powerful public statement. After the funeral, no public events were allowed in Galway until the end of the war. The *Connacht Tribune*'s increasingly militant tone is underlined by their printing of the guilty sentences handed down to King George V, Lloyd George, and the commander of the British Forces in Ireland by a Sinn Féin court deliberating on Griffin's murder. Afterwards, the manager of the paper and a reporter were taken from the office, blindfolded and threatened at gunpoint as a warning to avoid such seditious material in the future.[64] The labour movement also faced increasing repression, and in November the ITGWU premises in Galway was burned down, its leader forced to leave the city, and the wearing of the unions badge deemed to be illegal.[65] The 1,500-strong branch was suppressed, but its members were not. The British forces had by now totally lost control, and in an effort to wrest back the initiative, large numbers of Volunteers were rounded up and brought to Earl's Island in the city, where conditions were poor – '33 of us were given 32 blankets and herded in an old hut without glass in the only window, and never got a cup, knife or fork.'[66] A failure to achieve anything of use from these men led to all being released, ready to begin the cycle again.

A particularly horrifying event took place on 26 November as two brothers – Henry and Patrick Loughnane from Shanaglish – were arrested by the RIC and handed over to the Auxiliaries. The Auxiliaries visited their mother three days later to inform her that they had escaped from Drimharsna Castle. Nothing more was heard until 6 December, when their bodies were found in a pond in Drombriste. They had been badly tortured – 'Patrick's back was the only part of his body that was not blackened by burns ... Henry's body was scorched all over. Their arms and legs were broken and their faces were blown away.'[67] These events reflected the growing violence in November, matched elsewhere in the country – it was the bloodiest month of the conflict. Although each of these incidents generated great media exposure they were over-shadowed by the events of Bloody Sunday in Dublin on 21 November.

As the escalation continued, there were calls for peace. On 3 December, Galway County Council passed a resolution proclaiming its loyalty to the Dáil, but calling on all sides to agree a truce: 'We therefore, as adherents of Dáil Éireann, request that body to appoint three delegates who will have power to arrange a truce and preliminary terms of peace, so that an end may be brought to the unfortunate strife by a peace honourable to both countries.'[68] Although not an isolated attempt at peace at this time, it was the most public. As such, it was taken seriously by the British, and considered at a cabinet meeting on 6 December. The meeting decided that peace was desirable and there was a 'general agreement' over the removal of the ban on Dáil Éireann provided there was a cessation of hostilities. However, a decision could not be made until consultation took place with Hamar Greenwood, Chief Secretary for Ireland.[69] He convinced the cabinet to stay put and pursue a hard line, and the chance for peace was gone. The County Council's resolution remains controversial, and should not be taken to be indicative of local Sinn Féin opinion. Michael Collins was furious, as Lloyd George considered it a sign of the wilting of the Volunteers.[70] Many of the Council members were not present at the meeting, owing to imprisonment, and in Councillor Walsh's case, murder. Attending had become difficult, as several councillors were marked men and could not be present, and some have even cast doubt on whether the resolution was passed at all.[71] Pádraig Kilkelly, a member of the Council, asked Pádraig Ó Fathaigh to 'draw up a statement denouncing the resolution and pointing out that the great majority of the Co. Council were marked me[n] and could not attend the council meetings.'[72] It became known by local Volunteers as the 'White Feather Resolution' – they were extremely unhappy with it and anxious to prove incorrect the perception that 'turbulent Galway had been tamed'.[73]

The taming of Connacht was high on the minds of IRA GHQ, who openly pleaded with the west to do more in *An tÓglach* in February 1921.[74] Violence continued and even spread to places where previously there had been no action. John Geoghegan, Quartermaster of the East Connemara brigade and a district councillor, was shot despite 'no ambush [having] taken place in the district.'[75] The reorganization of brigades continued to have an effect. The West Connemara brigade was conscious of their combined lack of action over the preceding two years and being newly formed was now 'anxious for a good fight to justify our existence as a fighting unit.'[76] They engaged the RIC in a long gun fight at Mounterowen, and while the action was not successful, it helped to divert pressure away from the more active eastern part of the county, as in the aftermath of the fight, 'more than 1,000 troops and police … with planes to guide them' launched a round-up in the area.[77] In the meantime, the IRA had complete control of the countryside and continued to destroy the vestiges and symbols of British rule by attacking evacuated country houses, barracks and any buildings which could be useful to the British Army.[78]

Thomas Whelan, a native of the town of Clifden, was executed in Mountjoy prison in March 1921, triggering agitation in the town. One RIC man was killed, with another severely wounded. Reprisal was not long in coming, with a special train from Galway bringing Black and Tans who set fire to most of the principal houses in the town, killing a young ex-sergeant major and wounding an ex-RIC man.

Near misses and bad planning continued to characterize the conflict, as when the notorious RIC man, Igoe, came down from Dublin. GHQ informed local leaders that it wanted him dead, but they had to go Castlebar to get the required 'revolvers and bombs' needed to take on his well-armed convoy.[79] By the time they got back he had left.

There were two major events in 1921 prior to the truce. An IRA ambush by the South Galway/East Clare IRA at the gates of Ballyturin House, near Gort, Co. Galway resulted in the killing of District Inspector Cecil Blake, his wife and two British Army officers – Capt. Cornwallis and Lt. McCreery. Mrs Robert Gregory (Lady Gregory's daughter-in-law), also part of the party, was released unharmed by the Volunteers. When police and military arrived at the scene, a shot rang out killing RIC Constable John Kearney.[80] Strangely, given the relatively high ranking of the Army and RIC men, there was no retaliation, perhaps indicating the perception that a truce was not far away. This may be the reason some historians have given it little attention – Lyons erroneously described it as the 'massacre of a harmless tennis party.'[81] In March three murders in the city shocked many locals – 'two sick police sergeants lying in their beds in a hospital were deliberately shot dead by four masked men, and a civilian lying in the workhouse ward was similarly murdered. A sick police constable was wounded.'[82] The policemen, neither of whom had been expected to live, were shot in St Bride's Home on Sea Road. The civilian was in the workhouse hospital on account of gunshot wounds obtained during an attack on his property by masked men a fortnight previously.[83] Brutality was now commonplace and these incidents warranted less space in the local papers than lesser incidents in previous years.

Michael Brennan, head of the East Clare IRA, arrived later in May to reorganize the Clare and South Galway brigades under the command of the First Western Division.[84] He took control of the area of Galway south of the railway line from Galway to Ballinasloe. His first instruction was

> to go at once to south Galway and endeavour to get a Volunteer organization established there. According to GHQ the old brigades in south Galway had completely collapsed and I would find very little on which to work. I knew from our march through Galway that the material there was excellent and all that was needed was an organization with the right man in charge of the various units.[85]

Because of the proximity of his arrival to the calling of the truce on 11 July, Brennan had little impact on operations, and many of the companies were, in actual fact, well organized in any case.[86] His appointment however highlighted the increasing role Dublin played in the conflict.[87] Even the calling of the truce was beset by communication problems, Tomás Ó Máille recalling, 'ní raibh a fhios againn gur cuireadh teachtaire as Baile Átha Cliath chuig gach uile bhuíon in Éirinn a bhí ag troid, le hordú a thabhairt dóibh teacht suas ar an sos agus gan é a bhriseadh. [We didn't know that a message had been sent from Dublin to every company that was to fight giving an order to adhere to the truce and not to break it.]'[88]

The Volunteers were not active in Galway on the same level that they were in Cork, Kerry and elsewhere. They were nonetheless an important cog in the wheel, and success should not be determined solely by arbitrary rates of violence over the period. They contained a large military force in the county, both by the lingering threat of violence and agitation, sometimes enacted, and by an 'emerging intelligence gap'.[89] The IRA decisively won the intelligence war in Galway. Padraic Ó Fáthaigh, Joe Togher and others ensured that the Volunteers were well informed, and ahead of the British forces. Ó Fáthaigh was arrested in 1920 and although he was carrying a notebook detailing every IRA member and their arms in each district in both Irish and shorthand, the RIC could decode neither.[90] In contrast, Joe Togher spent most of the conflict intercepting RIC and British Army mail and despatches through his position at the GPO in Galway, even after officials suspected there was a breach of security: 'In order to enter the office at night, which I could not do officially, I was obliged to climb in through a second floor window, extract any mail I was doubtful about, bring them back home, break up the cipher and pass on the information to the Brigade Commandant, Seamus Murphy.'[91]

By 1920, the Galway RIC was receiving no information from the people, as informers were now widely regarded as traitors to their country.[92] The success of the Volunteers intelligence in Galway should not be overstated, but it certainly allowed for a severe curtailing of British forces ability to counteract them. All too often the same people were arrested, as the RIC blindly tried to gather information. Large-scale arrests were common, but rarely yielded much. They knew the organization of the Volunteers from above but not from within and decisively lost the intelligence battle in Galway.

Despite this, no real action was taken in response to much of the information received by the Volunteers. Togher obtained names and addresses of the Auxiliaries in Galway, but nothing was done.[93] Togher claimed with justification that he did not get the support needed from his comrades in Dublin and Galway to carry out such a plan and without cooperation he was left 'completely helpless.'[94] Gilbert Morrissey and others agreed with him – the leadership in the county was poor. Ultimately, 'Connacht Volunteers were willing to defy the police, but violence was sporadic.'[95] A number of London Irish wanted to come to the south of Galway to try and form a flying column but were told by locals it was arms and not men that were needed, and yet when Pádraic Ó Fáthaigh tried to form a column himself he ran into difficulty getting the required manpower. As a result Ó Fathaigh and Willie Hynes left to join the mid-Clare brigade flying column.[96] Pride alone prevented the London Irishmen from joining the fight in Galway.

The influence of the clergy was important, but 'Episcopal authority [was] far from absolute' in Galway.[97] Prior to the Rising Tom Kenny had been seen by the police as having similar authority to the Church hierarchy in the east of the county.[98] Anti-violence sermons were republished in newspapers, and while these carried weight, it was often with the merchant classes rather than local Volunteers. The priests often reflected the opinion of the community rather than influencing it in one way or another. There were clergy who supported the volunteers, but equally, other clergy denounced violence.

The period of the War of Independence in Galway is characterized by its variety. It oscillated between economic and political factors, between quiet and violent periods. Ultimately, Galway played its part in the struggle, but it was a relatively minor role. The reasons for IRA inactivity are various. Despite Fitzpatrick's assertion that leadership was not an overly important issue, it proved to be so in Galway. One of the reasons the Rising had taken place in the county was leadership, as opposed to the situation in Limerick: 'the Galway Volunteers … facing an almost identical set of circumstances produced a very different result to Michael Colivet's Limerick due largely to the direction of Liam Mellows.'[99] Mellows was elected for Galway, but was not in the county much after the Rising, and his absence, along with others, left a large vacuum. When Galway was reorganized, a more efficient and active IRA resulted. Chronic arms shortages also played a part, as did bad luck – 'several ambushes

9 Eglinton Canal, 1920

were prepared for the RIC but they did not oblige by turning up at the required time' – this is a recurring complaint.[1] The sheer number of crown forces was important. Joe Togher estimated there were 2,000 in the city alone, which was the headquarters for the region. That equates to more than one for every seven citizens.[2] The Black and Tans were stationed in Eglinton Street, Dominick Street, the docks and Salthill. The Auxiliaries were in Lenaboy, Taylors Hill and The Retreat, Salthill. A battalion of 4th Worcester's were stationed at the Workhouse, the 17th Lancers at Earl's Island, and the Connaught Rangers and general mixed infantry at Renmore barracks, making the armed British presence in the city suffocating. The economic circumstances, prevalent countrywide, were acute in the west of the county, where localized famines played an important role and chronic food shortages forced national independence to become secondary to survival.

The causes of one county's activity or inactivity during the period are many and varied, and as Hart and Fitzpatrick have alluded to in their geographical studies of the period, different for each county. Research carried out on the geography of militancy in the period has been done on a county-by-county basis but that is not an accurate barometer of violence, as it does not reflect bias within any county, particularly when the county is as comparatively large as Galway. It was divided into two ridings for administrative purposes by the British, and into several divisions by the IRA. To treat is as one unit when neither of the belligerents treated it as such is therefore fraught with difficulty. Galway was hugely diverse as the period showed. Most of the action was in the east and south of the county, the economically more prosperous area, while the poorer west was dormant for much of the period.

4. The Civil War, 1922–3

On 7 January 1922, Dáil Éireann narrowly approved the Anglo-Irish treaty, a decision which was ratified by the public on 18 June. Pro-Treaty Sinn Féin achieved 239,193 votes while Anti-Treaty Sinn Féin won 133,864. All other votes (247,226) out of a valid poll of 620,283 went to Pro-Treaty parties, predominantly Labour, the Farmers Party, and Independents.[1] 78.42 per cent of the electorate supported the treaty, 21.58 per cent did not.

The results in Galway, now a single constituency with seven seats instead of four separate constituencies as in 1918, was not as conclusive, but a consensus nonetheless emerged. Pro-Treaty Sinn Féin and Labour combined for 24,717 votes or 67.7 per cent while Anti-Treaty Sinn Féin managed 11,780 or 32.2 per cent, significantly higher than their national norm.[2] Despite this, and the election of two TDs, Frank Fahy and Bryan Cusack, the Anti-Treaty side lost one of its most high profile members in the Dáil when Liam Mellows failed to be returned. The leader of the 1916 Rising in Galway, he was one of the more eloquent voices against the treaty. It was regarded as 'the most severe blow for republicans' in the entire campaign, one which also saw the loss of Constance Markievicz and Erskine Childers.[3] Galway voters were more divided than their national counterparts, but not as deeply as other counties where the civil war was to be particularly violent, such as Kerry and Cork.[4]

The timing of this vote and its emphatic Pro-Treaty message did not avoid further bloodshed. From April onwards a garrison opposed to the treaty occupied the Four Courts in Dublin and, after months of inaction, Collins shelled their position. The dynamic of the Civil War was largely the same as the 1919–21 conflict, with guerrilla warfare dominant in concentrated areas of the country. It has often been suggested that the only change the treaty achieved was that of the uniforms.[5] Little changed after the British pull-out other than the intensity of the violence. Some counties experienced fierce fighting where there had been little before, notably Sligo.[6]

Limerick provided the scene for conflict before the war began properly. Both pro- and anti-treaty factions wanted to occupy the barracks the British Army was evacuating. In March Richard Mulcahy ordered Michael Brennan and Free State troops from the 1st Western Division, which now included substantial numbers of Galwaymen, to enter Limerick City and take the barracks.[7] Mulcahy underestimated the ease with which they would do so and Brennan found himself surrounded and 'hopelessly under resourced'.[8] Many of the men under his command had not fought in the War of Independence.

Cumann na Saoirse

POINTS FOR CANVASSERS

The Treaty rids us of—

(1) The British Army, the instrument of British power in Ireland.

(2) A police force trained for political espionage.

(3) British control of education, which was killing the Irish language and destroying the soul of the nation.

(4) British legislation.

(5) British officialdom which ran the Government of Ireland for the benefit of England.

(6) British control of our purse, and British taxation which left Ireland the one country in Europe with a decreasing population.

(7) The stranglehold of Britain on Irish trade and industry.

The Treaty gives us—

(1) An Irish Regular Army, with modern equipment, sworn to the service of Ireland.

(2) An Irish Police Force designed solely for the maintenance of law and order.

(3) Irish control of education, with power to restore the language and build up a national culture.

(4) An Irish Parliament with full power to make laws and subject to **NO** British veto.

(5) An Irish Executive subject only to the authority of the Irish Parliament.

(6) Power to develop the resources and industries of Ireland, and to stop the drain of emigration.

(7) The raising and spending of our own revenue.

MAHON'S PRINTING WORKS, DUBLIN.

10 Pro-Treaty election pamphlet, 1922

He made two agreements with Liam Lynch to avoid conflict, but these deals were repudiated by Dublin, and the situation did not resolve itself for months. Much of South Galway was thus left unguarded, and there were several ambushes of Free State troops bound for Limerick as they marched south.[9]

Galway did not follow the national trend however, as the Civil War failed to match the War of Independence in its intensity. Little of note occurred in the field, but there was a marked difference in the treatment of prisoners, leading to several deaths. This was due to the legislation passed by the new government in September 1922. Commonly referred to as the Public Safety Bill, in effect it enacted martial law.[10] Men carrying arms against the state could now be summarily executed – an action which was to leave a bitter aftertaste in national and local politics in the decades following the war.

The clergy, most of whom were openly Pro-Treaty, contributed significantly to the low intensity of military action in Galway. Many priests, particularly younger ones, had been involved at all levels of the War of Independence.[11] Their political allegiance undoubtedly had an effect on their parishioners. When Mellows was canvassing before the election on 16 June 1922, 'special attention was paid to influential priests'.[12] Their role should not be overstated, as the clergy was generally Pro-Treaty nationwide, and events did not play out as benignly in other parts of the country as was the case in Galway.

The Civil War proper began on 28 June 1922. Of the three IRA divisions in Galway, the 1st Western Division was pro-treaty while the 2nd and 4th Western were anti-treaty. In late June the National Army entered the city, which was surrounded by Anti-treaty forces. In the city both sides had areas of strength. Brennan's 1st Western Division occupied the county jail, the courthouse and the Railway Hotel, while anti-treatyites initially held Eglinton Street barracks and minor buildings. Although a tentative truce was quickly agreed, the anti-treatyites evacuated the city in July, burning many buildings behind them. They attempted an attack on the city in the following days, but were easily rebuffed.[13]

After several days fighting, the irregulars retreated from the city, burning buildings as they left, including Renmore barracks. On 30 June a protestant orphanage was burnt down by anti-treaty forces in Clifden.[14] A destroyer was ordered to Galway, and transferred the 58 orphan children who had been resident there, to England, pointing to the impotence of the Free State army in Connemara at the time.[15] It is the most prominent example of sectarianism rising to the fore in Galway. There were instances of land seizures as religious reprisals, but they were isolated and the work of individuals.[16] In a society where people had grown accustomed to taking the law into their own hands, it is unsurprising old scores would be settled, this time against a community known in the past for its proselytizing.[17] Predictably, it generated significant coverage, with Edward Carson describing as 'one of the very worst [cases] of the many hundreds that had been sent to him within the past two months'.[18]

Food supplies were seriously affected in the city and the west of the county. They normally arrived by road and rail, but there were road blocks on the main routes, and most railway bridges had been blown up. In an effort to provide relief and to secure support for the new government the Dáil voted large amounts of money for relief to the west.[19] These relief funds were poorly administered by a government with little experience. In Letterfrack the local parish priest, Fr Godfrey became exasperated at delays in receiving monies and foodstuffs. The area had been obtaining relief on an annual basis for several years, but delays in 1922 nearly proved fatal.[20] A nationwide post office strike was dealt with brutally by the new government, who refused the workers' offer of a 12.5 per cent pay cut, and instead arrested the strike leaders in Galway.[21] Issues like this distanced the locals from the Free State, and made it difficult for the government to make inroads in the predominantly anti-treaty west of the county.

In October an attack from anti-treaty forces from Connemara on Clifden resulted in the town being taken after a long fight.[22] Such actions were the exception in Galway – there were raids and small-scale scuffles, but few major incidents. The leader of the 2nd Western Brigade of the IRA, Comdt. Thomas Maguire put this down to war weariness and a lack of enthusiasm for engagement, stating very simply that 'There was a different feeling altogether. The British were the enemy, the old enemy; there was a certain pride in having the ability to attack them. That feeling was entirely absent in the Civil War.'[23] As well as war weariness, Maguire cited a lack of 'cohesion or military council formed between the provincial commanders here'.[24] There was no appetite for conflict in Galway. Despite this eleven IRA prisoners were executed. These executions did little to change the war, and did not provoke much immediate response. In contrast, they poisoned politics for decades.

On 20 January 1923, five men were executed in Athlone as a result of the aforementioned state policy. Four were from north county Galway: Martin Bourke, Stephen Joyce, Herbert Collins and Michael Walsh. The fifth man, Thomas Hughes, from Athlone, Co. Westmeath, was attached to the North Galway Brigade. On 19 February, eighteen volunteers were arrested by Free State forces in Annaghdown. One, John Francis Rattigan of Caherlistrane, escaped, but the others were brought to Galway Jail. A Free State bulletin telling of their capture declared all were well armed.[25] Despite this however, there were no casualties, implying increasing war weariness. The number of arrests made it increasingly difficult for the irregulars to operate and matters were soon to come to a head.

In March 1923 in Roscommon a meeting was held for anti-treaty Brigade O/Cs in the Western Command areas. All present were asked to select one target and, in a coherent move, attack as a last effort. The war was drawing to a close, and most of the O/Cs either ignored the order, or chose not to act. The exception was the 2nd Western Division, who attacked Headford barracks.

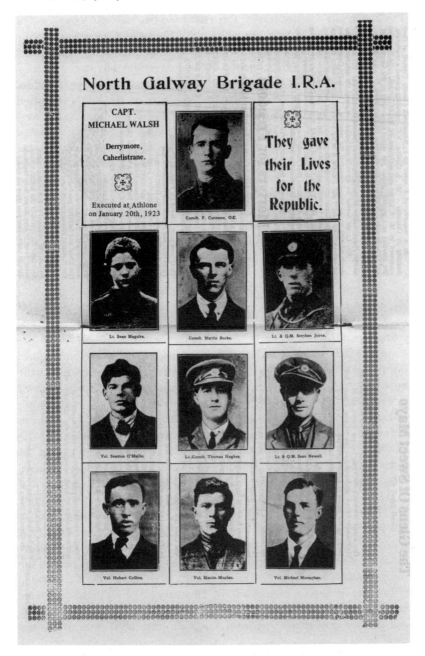

11 Anti-Treaty Galwaymen executed by the Free State

The action was a failure, leaving three dead and one seriously wounded. On the IRA side, John Higgins was killed, while Daniel McCormack was to die several years later as a result of his wounds.[26] Two Free State soldiers died during the attack. The consequences of the engagement did not end there.

Tuam, very near to Caherlistrane, provided the setting for further executions on 24 April that same year, when Francis Cunnane (Headford), Michael Monaghan (Headford), Martin Moylan (Annaghdown), John Maguire (Galway) James (or John) Newell (Galway) and James O'Malley (Oughterard) were shot and killed. The men were arbitrarily picked to send a message to anti-treatyites that any further military actions against the state would have the most serious possible repercussions. There were several more condemned to death who avoided the firing squad. Among them was Jim Cradock, who after initially being told he was to die, saw another picked in his place. Cradock later told his son that this man was 'young, very frightened, and he felt terrible about it'.[27] Although not officially related to the attack in Headford, the proximity of the two events makes this highly likely as a reprisal. All the men were part of the 2nd Western Division, under the command of Commandant General Tom Maguire at the time of the executions. These were the final actions of the war in Galway which ended on 24 May 1923, with the Anti-Treaty side badly beaten. It had proven a pointless conflict, accomplishing little, but changing much and embittering many.

In a similar pattern to the War of Independence in the county, the war had been waged at a low level of intensity, yet resulted in events which were important on a national scale. Seventy-seven men were summarily executed by Free State forces during the conflict, eleven of whom were from the North Galway Brigade.[28] This is clearly disproportionate to the scale of events in Galway, and when taken in the national context is most surprising. The fact that there was no subsequent upsurge in violence is also unusual, given the tit-for-tat nature of violence previously. Although the executions were horrific they did not exacerbate the situation.[29] The appetite for war was gone.

Though the war was over, there was no immediate release of prisoners, with many detained in Galway Jail until late June 1924.[30] In commenting upon this, the *Connacht Tribune* stated the release 'would be generally welcomed' and it would 'close forever the most miserable and sordid page in Ireland's history.'[31] There was little else in the way of violent political activity in the short, medium and long term in the county. Writings on the Civil War in Galway are sparse, as is source material. The main narratives of the period are contradictory about the fight in the west, there are few eyewitness statements, and the newspapers were censored, leading to inaccurate information and speculation.[32]

There had been 'widespread optimism that with the arrival of the new order western problems would be dramatically eliminated.'[33] The civil war was to prove this optimism wrong in the first years of the state, and it was to be

12 Staff at the Custom House, Galway, 1922

many years before genuine progress was made. The popular remembrance of the period has proven problematic and long lasting. In 1952 a plan emerged to erect a memorial gate by Seamus Murphy RHA on O'Brien's bridge in Galway City, bearing the inscription 'In honour of the men and women of Galway City and County who suffered for freedom during the years 1916–23.'[34] However, the inclusion of the Civil War years on the carving led to opposition and the project never completed, despite considerable enthusiasm.[35] Civil War wounds were still raw almost 30 years later, and even when mooted again in 1975 the passing of 50 years still had not removed the bitterness. This was the case even though Galway bucked the national trend, and saw less bloodshed during the Civil War than in the War of Independence. A war between brothers is easier to remember and more difficult to forget.

Conclusion

The period 1910–23 was a momentous and violent period in the history of Galway, and one which changed it forever. British forces no longer occupied its towns and villages, but the Civil War that followed their withdrawal made celebration of the period problematic. There was independence of a kind, but many of the same old problems remained. Emigration, the scourge of the island, was reduced from 1914–23, but soon returned to hit the west of Ireland with an intensity unequalled in much of the rest of the country. Many of the social problems evident in Galway prior to and during our period were still present; social unrest, small holdings, poor farming practices, the lack of a sustained middle class. Problems inherent in a state of violence for five years also existed, with the infrastructure of the county and the country badly damaged. The persistent existence of these difficulties allowed for renewed emigration, and a vicious cycle was re-established.

It is tempting therefore to ask what exactly had changed in a day-to-day sense. True, land reform by 1923 was virtually complete, and what still needed reformation was seen to by the Land Reform Commission set up that year. The British had left 26 of Ireland's counties, excepting the Treaty ports. Yet the new administration was in many respects as conservative in its attitudes to class and economics as what had preceded it, possibly even more so, loath as it would be to admit it.[1] The sweeping reforms promised in the proclamations of Independence of 1916 and 1918 were not delivered for some time, and in some cases not at all. The Free State, subsequently Éire, and later the Republic of Ireland, fostered a stilted cultural growth. Many of the country's great writers felt obliged to leave. Strict censorship was the order of the day. While in many respects culturally bankrupt, the new state did not fare any better economically. It stabilized itself admirably prior to the Wall Street Crash of 1929 without changing radically, but ultimately it took until the 1960s and subsequently 1990s for sustained but limited periods of growth. Emigration continued and the population dropped. These musings about the State post-1923 were in many cases amplified in the west of the country, including Galway. Yet despite this catalogue of misfortune, the period of revolution which gave the country its freedom was absolutely revered. Ironically, it was the outbreak of the Troubles in Northern Ireland that caused brakes to be put on this runaway hagiography. The advent of revolutionary violence, particularly in its uglier forms from the 1980s onwards, led to discomfort at the thought of it in some way legitimizing that violence by remembering the War of Independence in any fond way. In many respects this is to be admired because it led to, as Diarmuid Ferriter put it, 'the dethroning of heroes', something valuable not for its own sake, but crucial for the ability to view the period in a more objective way.[2]

Yet despite this, there was still often an historical agenda, albeit an understandable one. To glamorize contemporary violence when looking at the events of the past is still a barrier to completely objective analysis. To avoid attaching such glamour to the Provisional IRA's campaign in the north, the government of the Republic of Ireland went so far as to have no celebration of the 70th anniversary of the Rising. To this end the BBC's Kevin Connolly noted in 2006 that 'most people in Ireland draw a moral and political distinction between the activities of the "old" IRA in the 1920s and those of the Provisional IRA in the 1970s and 1980s but there was a general feeling that a military march past might have blurred that distinction.'[3] With the end of the conflict in the north, and the opening of the Bureau of Military History's witness statements, there is now an opportunity to reassess the period.

Much of what happened in Galway from 1910 to 1923 has been largely forgotten. Yet it provides a most interesting case study, both in the local and national context. Local commanders had much power, as was the case elsewhere, but unlike certain other counties they often refused to use it. Friction between localities and local brigades was prevalent, but again was also visible elsewhere.[4] The geography of the county provided a variety of features: mountains and hills, lowlands, plains, good quality land, poor land, lakes etc. The issue of the Irish language is one instance in which Galway cannot be said to be typical of the country as a whole, though counties with high levels of fighting such as Clare, Cork and Kerry also had many native Irish speakers amongst their respective populations.

It may have had more extreme poverty and land issues than some of its neighbours, and a class structure that was not prevalent everywhere else, but Galway was not unique. The problem is trying to define Galway as a unit of study in a local versus national context. While this may be natural because of its political and historical boundaries, the vast majority of action took place in the eastern part of the county, including the city. This illustrates the difficulty of taking the inflexible county as the unit of study.

Ultimately, the experience of Galway during the revolutionary years was paradoxical. The county's prevalence as a centre of agitation and a hive of Sinn Féin activity marked it out as one of the most unstable counties in the country, a label which it never lived up to. It played a minor role in the outcome of the revolution, but an important role nonetheless. Due to its comparative inactivity when compared with other counties in this way it has been neglected as a source of research. Yet the county faced massive upheaval during this period, politically, socially and economically and has only recently emerged from its shadow. These factors all combined to create the revolution as it happened in Galway. The scope of that revolution may have been small, but it does not deserve to be forgotten.

NOTES

ABBREVIATIONS

JGHAS   *Journal of the Galway Historical and Archaeological Society*
MA   Military Archives
TNA   The National Archives, London

INTRODUCTON

1 See Fergus Campbell, *Land and revolution: nationalist politics in the west of Ireland, 1891–1921* (Oxford, 2005).

2 David Fitzpatrick, 'The geography of Irish nationalism 1910–1921', *Past and Present*, 78 (Feb. 1978), 117.

3 See Maurice Walsh, *The news from Ireland: foreign correspondents and the Irish revolution* (London, 2008).

I. GATHERING STORM CLOUDS, 1910–16

1 W.E.Vaughan & A.J. Fitzpatrick (eds), *Irish historical statistics: population, 1821–1971* (Dublin, 1978), p. 14.

2 *Annual report of the registrar general for Ireland containing a general abstract of the numbers of marriages, births And deaths registered in Ireland during the year 1910*, HC, 1911 [Cd. 5783] p. 18.

3 Ibid. In 1910, the excess of births over deaths in Mayo was 2,042 while the figure for Galway was only 1,390.

4 Virginia Crossman, 'Middle class attitudes to poverty and welfare in post-famine Ireland' in Fintan Lane (ed.), *Politics, society and the middle class in modern Ireland* (London, 2010), p. 138.

5 *Census of Ireland, 1911. Province of Connaught, County of Galway* HC 1912–13 [Cd. 6052] cxvii p. vii.

6 Timothy P. O'Neill, 'Minor famines and relief in County Galway, 1815–1925' in Gerard Moran (ed.), *Galway: history and society* (Dublin, 1996) p. 472.

7 Barry R. O'Brien, *Dublin Castle and the Irish people* (London, 1909), p. 52.

8 Fitzpatrick, 'The geography of Irish nationalism', p. 142.

9 Campbell, *Land and revolution*, p. 85.

10 David Fitzpatrick, *Politics and Irish life, 1913–1921 – provincial experience of war and rebellion* (Aldershot, 1993), p. 2.

11 Arthur Lynch, 'The moral of the Galway election', *The New Liberal Review* (London, 1902), p. 860.

12 As quoted in Margaret Digby, *Horace Plunkett: an Anglo American Irishman* (Oxford, 1949), p. 93.

13 Willliam O'Malley, *Glancing back* (London, n.d. [1933]), pp 171–2.

14 Caitriona Clear, 'Homelessness, crime, punishment and poor relief in Galway 1850–1914: an introduction', *JGAHS*, 50 (1998), 130.

15 John Cunningham, '*A town tormented by the Sea': Galway 1790–1914* (Dublin, 2004), p. 39.

16 Michael Myers Shoemaker, *Wanderings in Ireland* (New York & London, 1908), pp 97–8.

17 See Timothy Collins, *Transatlantic triumph and heroic failure: the story of the Galway line* (Cork, 2002).

18 Cunningham, '*A town tormented by the sea*', p. 2.

19 Ibid., p. 4.

20 Ibid.

21 There had been some precedence for Labour in Galway – there were frequent strikes on the Galway–Clifden rail line, as well as a short newspaper boys strike in 1911, but these were low level and short lived.

22 Cunningham, '*A town tormented by the sea*', p. 241

23 Mary Clancy, 'On the western outpost; local government and women's suffrage in Co. Galway 1898–1918' in Moran (ed.), *Galway: history and society*, p. 557.

24 *Connacht Tribune*, 9 May 1909.

25 Ibid., 22 May 1909.

26 *Congested Districts Board for Ireland: nineteenth report* [CD. 5712] (Dublin, 1911), p. 8.

27 Cormac Ó Gráda, *Ireland before and after the famine: explorations in economic history: 1800–1925* (Manchester, 1993), pp 181–2. Ó Gráda mentions a case in Kerry, but it is safe to assume that the same could be said of some of the more isolated parts of Connemara.

28 Joseph Lee, *The modernisation of Irish society, 1848–1918* (Dublin, 2008), pp 103–4.

29 Thomas Bartlett, *Ireland: a history* (Cambridge, 2010), p. 318.

30 *Galway Observer*, 22 Jan. 1910.

31 O'Neill, 'Minor famines and relief in County Galway', p. 471.

32 *Connacht Tribune*, 17 June 1911.

33 The exception to this is Ballinasloe, which actually had a negative excess of births over deaths in 1911.

34 *Congested Districts Board For Ireland: nineteenth report* [CD. 5712] (Dublin, 1911), p. 6.

35 Lee, *The modernisation of Irish society*, p. 128.

36 Some of the towns increased in size, as we have seen, but migration was not a prominent feature of Galway demographics.

37 David Fitzpatrick, 'Militarism in Ireland, 1900–1922' in Thomas Bartlett & Keith Jeffery (eds), *A military history of Ireland* (Cambridge, 1996), p. 379.

38 Gilbert Morrissey witness statement, MA, BMH WS 1138.

39 *Connacht Tribune*, 13 Aug. 1910.

40 Tony Varley, 'A region of sturdy smallholders?: western nationalists and agrarian politics during the First World War', *JGAHS*, 55 (2003), 134.

41 Ibid.

42 *Connacht Tribune*, 29 Oct. 1910 & *Connacht Tribune*, 24 Dec. 1910.

43 Ibid., 17 Dec. 1910.

44 Ibid., 8 Oct. 1910.

45 *Galway Observer*, 24 Feb. 1912

46 Campbell, *Land and revolution*, p. 185.

47 Michael Manning witness statement, MA, BMH WS 1164.

48 Campbell, *Land and revolution*, p. 173.

49 Ibid., p. 185.

50 Eugene Duggan, *The ploughman on the pound note: farmer politics in County Galway in the twentieth century* (Athenry, 2004), p. 30. Finnerty had been a founder of the UIL in Galway originally.

51 Campbell, *Land and revolution*, p. 183.

52 Ibid., p. 190.

53 *Connacht Tribune*, 1 Jan. 1910 – declares that the IPP has the unwavering support of the clergy.

54 Paul Bew, *Ireland: the politics of enmity, 1789–2006* (Oxford, 2007), pp 367–8.

55 John Hosty witness statement, MA, BMH WS 373.

56 Fearghal McGarry, *The Rising, Ireland: Easter 1916* (Oxford, 2010), p. 54 & Frank Hardiman private papers. McGarry gives a far lower figure, likely based on the *Royal Commission on the rebellion*, but Hardiman's is more likely to be correct, as he owned the Town Hall and was heavily involved in the Volunteers organization.

57 Michael Manning witness statement, MA, BMH WS 1164.

58 *Connacht Tribune*, 3 Oct. 1914.

59 Campbell, *Land and revolution*, pp 193–5.

60 John Hosty witness statement, MA, BMH WS 373.

61 Thomas Courtney witness statement, MA, BMH WS 447.

62 Siobhán Meagher-Phelan, 'The changing face of Irish nationalist politics 1910–1921: an examination of the evidence from Galway' (MA Thesis, UCG, 1989), p. 8.

63 *Connacht Tribune*, 17 June 1916. See also *Connacht Tribune* frequently 1914–17.

64 H.D. Gribbon, 'Economic and social history, 1850–1921' in W.E. Vaughan (ed.), *A new history of Ireland: vi: Ireland under the Union, II: 1870–1921* (Oxford, 1996), p. 347.

65 *Galway Express*, 29 Aug. 1914.

66 John Hosty witness statement, MA, BMH WS 373.

67 Frank Hardiman private papers.

68 Fitzpatrick, 'Militarism in Ireland', p. 379.

69 Patrick Treacy witness statement, MA, BMH WS 1425.

70 Michael Hynes witness statement, MA, BMH WS 1173.

71 Inspector Rutledge, as quoted in *The Royal Commission on the rebellion in Ireland* [Cd. 8311] (London, HMSO, 1916), p. 77.
72 Campbell, *Land and revolution*, p. 198.
73 William Henry, *Forgotten heroes: Galway soldiers of the Great War, 1914–1918* (Cork, 2007), p. 32; Victor Whitmarsh, *Shadows on glass: Galway, 1895–1960, a pictorial record* (Galway, n.d. [2000]), p. 115. Whitmarsh reached the figure of 755 from Ireland's Memorial Records compiled by the committee of the Irish National War Memorial.

2. THE RISING AND ITS AFTERMATH, 1916–18

1 W.E. Vaughan & A.J. Fitzpatrick (eds), *Irish historical statistics: population, 1821–1971* (Dublin, 1978).
2 Varley, 'A region of sturdy smallholders?', pp 131–2.
3 Ibid., p. 134.
4 Ibid.
5 Frances Moffett, *I also am of Ireland* (London, 1985), p. 83.
6 Ibid.
7 Fitzpatrick, 'Militarism in Ireland, 1900–1922', p. 399.
8 *The Royal Commission on the Rebellion in Ireland*, [Cd. 8311], (London, HMSO, 1916) p. 109.
9 Patrick Callanan witness statement, MA, BMH WS 405.
10 As quoted in Campbell, *Land and revolution*, p. 193.
11 Campbell, *Land and revolution*, p. 202.
12 Proinsias Ó hEidhin as quoted in Éamonn Ó'hEochaidh, *Liam Mellows* (Liam Mellows Cumann of Sinn Féin, Dublin, 1975), p. 3.
13 Very Revd Dr Thomas Fahy witness statement, MA, BMH WS 383.
14 Inspector Rutledge, as quoted in *The Royal Commission on the Rebellion in Ireland*, p. 75.
15 Patrick Callanan witness statement, MA, BMH WS 405.
16 James McGuire & James Quinn (eds), *Dictionary of Irish biography from the earliest times to the year 2002*, vol. V (Cambridge, 2010), pp 477–9.
17 Patrick Callanan witness statement, MA, BMH WS 405.
18 Ibid.
19 Ibid.
20 McGarry, *The Rising* , p. 220.
21 Pádraic Ó Fathaigh & Timothy McMahon (eds), *Pádraic Ó Fathaigh's War of Independence: recollections of a Galway Gaelic Leaguer* (Cork, 2000), p. 35.
22 As quoted in Fergus Campbell, 'The Easter Rising in Galway', *History Ireland* (March/April 2006), 25.
23 James McCarra private correspondence.
24 John Hosty witness statement, MA, BMH WS 373.
25 Patrick Callanan witness statement, MA, BMH WS 405.
26 Michael Ó Drioghneain witness statement, MA, BMH WS 374.
27 John D. Costello witness statement, MA, BMH WS 1330.
28 Frank Hardiman private papers.
29 Michael Hynes witness statement, MA, BMH WS 1173.
30 Campbell, 'Easter Rising in Galway', p. 23.
31 Patrick Callanan witness statement, MA, BMH WS 405.
32 Liam Nolan & John Nolan, *Secret victory: Ireland and the war at sea, 1914–1918* (Cork, 2009), p. 141.
33 *New York Times*, 4 May 1916.
34 Moffett, *I also am of Ireland*, p. 81.
35 Martin Newell witness statement, MA, BMH WS 1562.
36 Very Revd Dr Thomas Fahy witness statement, MA, BMH WS 383.
37 Martin Newell witness statement, MA, BMH WS 1562.
38 Michael Brennan, *The war in Clare, 1911–1921* (Dublin, 1984), p. 16.
39 Ibid.
40 *Connacht Tribune*, 29 Apr. 1916.
41 Ibid.
42 Frank Hardiman private papers.
43 *Connacht Tribune*, 6 May 1916.
44 Ibid., 22 July 1916.
45 Moffett, *I also am of Ireland* , p. 81
46 *Galway Observer*, 8 July 1916.
47 Ibid., & *Connacht Tribune*, 13 Aug. 1916.
48 CI Monthly Report, west Galway, May 1916, TNA, CO 904/100.
49 See Philip Bull, *Land, politics and nationalism: a study of the Irish land question* (Dublin, 1996)

50 Fitzpatrick, *Politics and Irish life*, p. 282.
51 Seán O'Mahony, *Frongoch: university of rebellion* (Dublin, 1987), p. 196. Only Dublin had more prisoners than Galway represented there. The story was similar in other prisons, such as Dartmoor, which took 65 prisoners from the rebellion, of whom 20 were from Galway: Ó Fathaigh & McMahon, *Pádraic Ó Fathaigh's War of Independence*, p. 42.
52 O'Mahony, *Frongoch*, pp 220–1.
53 Gilbert Morrissey witness statement, MA, BMH WS 1138.
54 Ibid.
55 *Irish Times*, 12 Mar. 1919.
56 *Connacht Tribune*, 4 Aug. 1917.
57 Brian M. Walker (ed.), *Parliamentary results in Ireland, 1918–92* (Dublin, 1992), p. 7.
58 Fitzpatrick, 'Geography of Irish nationalism', p. 124.
59 Thomas Nohilly witness statement, MA, BMH WS 1437.
60 Peter Hart, 'The geography of revolution in Ireland 1917–1923', *Past and Present*, 155 (May, 1997), 167. Fitzpatrick has also emphasized this, see Fitzpatrick, *Power and politics*.
61 Varley, 'A region of sturdy smallholders?', pp 136–40.

3. THE WAR OF INDEPENDENCE, 1919–21

1 *Galway Express*, 19 Jan. 1918; Liam Clune, 'The Galway Press and the Irish War of Independence, 1919–21' (MA Thesis, NUIG, 2007), p. 11.
2 *Connacht Tribune*, 31 Mar. 1918.
3 *Irish Times*, 12 Mar. 1919; Michael Hynes witness statement MA, BMH WS 1173.
4 Mícheál Ó Droighneáin witness statement, MA, BMH WS 1718.
5 *Connacht Tribune*, 5 Oct. 1918 & Joe Togher witness statement, MA, BMH WS 1718.
6 Diarmuid Ferriter, *The transformation of Ireland: 1900–2000* (London, 2004), p. 185; James Murray, *Galway: a medico-socio history* (Galway, 1993), p. 139.
7 John D. Costello witness statement. MA, BMH WS 1330.
8 *Irish Times*, 25 Apr. 1919.
9 Ibid., 7 Mar. 1919.
10 Ibid., 27 Aug. 1919. Campbell erroneously lists the attack on Loughgeorge barracks as the first engagement in his otherwise excellent chronology. Detailing it as 25 May 1919, it in fact occurred one year later. See *Irish Times*, 27 May 1920.
11 Gilbert Morrissey witness statement, MA, BMH WS 1138.
12 Ibid.
13 Ibid.
14 *Galway Express*, 10 Jan. 1920; John D. Costello witness statement. MA, BMH WS 1330.
15 *Galway Express*, 10 Apr. 1920.
16 Fergus Campbell (ed.); Kevin O'Shiel, 'The last land war? Kevin O'Shiel's memoir of the Irish Revolution', *Archivium Hibernicum*, 57 (2003), 155. Campbell suggests the agrarian violence between March and June of 1920 exceeded that in any year since 1882.
17 Cathal Brugha to Father Bourke, 21 Oct 1917, MA, BMH CD 161/2.
18 Varley, 'A region of sturdy smallholders?', p. 137.
19 H.B.C Pollard, *The secret societies of Ireland: their rise and progress* (London, 1920), p. 238.
20 Conor Kostick, *Revolution in Ireland: popular militancy, 1917–21* (Cork, 2009), p. 111.
21 Varley, 'A region of sturdy smallholders?', pp 131–4.
22 Clune, 'The Galway press and the Irish War of Independence, 1919–21', p. 13.
23 Patrick Treacy witness statement, MA, BMH WS 1426.
24 As quoted in Campbell, 'The last land war?', p. 163.
25 *Irish Times*, 22 Nov. 1966.
26 *Connacht Tribune*, 6 Mar. 1920.
27 Campbell, 'The last land war?', p. 167.
28 *Galway Express*, 1 May 1920.
29 J. Murphy (ed.), *Lady Gregory's Journals, Volume I, Books 1–29, 10 October 1916–24 February 1925* (Gerrards Cross, 1978), pp 68–229
30 As quoted in Campbell, 'The last land war?', p. 166.

31 Michael Manning witness statement, MA, BMH WS 1164.

32 Maryann Gialanella Valiulis, *Portrait of a revolutionary: General Richard Mulcahy and the founding of the Irish Free State* (Dublin, 1992), p. 57.

33 *Connacht Tribune*, 8 May 1920.

34 John Hosty witness statement, MA, BMH WS 373.

35 Gilbert Morrissey witness statement, MA, BMH WS 1138.

36 Kostick, *Revolution in Ireland*, p. 131.

37 *Galway Express*, 17 July 1920.

38 Richard Bennett, *The Black and Tans* (Kent, 2001) p. 110.

39 *Connacht Tribune*, 21 June 1919.

40 *Galway Observer*, 24 July 1920.

41 Ibid.

42 Ibid.

43 Douglas V. Duff, *Sword for hire: the saga of a modern free-companion* (London, 1934), p. 67.

44 Brennan, *The war in Clare*, p. 84.

45 Uinseann Mac Eoin (ed.), *Survivors* (Dublin, 1987), p. 428.

46 TNA, County Inspector Monthly Report, West Galway, Aug. 1920.

47 *Connacht Tribune*, 13 Sept. 1920.

48 Duff, *Sword for hire*, p. 77.

49 *Connacht Tribune*, 31 Jan. 1920 & 21 Aug. 1920.

50 Ibid., 3 Apr. 1920.

51 Ibid., 21 Aug. 1920.

52 Ibid., 23 Oct. 1920; Joe Togher witness statement, MA, BMH WS 1729.

53 *Galway Observer*, 6 Nov. 1920 & *Connacht Tribune*, 6 Nov. 1920.

54 *Connacht Tribune*, 11 Sept. 1920. See also Figure 6.

55 Joe Togher witness statement, MA, BMH WS 1729.

56 Ibid.

57 *Connacht Tribune*, 1 Dec. 1920.

58 Joe Togher witness statement, MA, BMH WS 1729.

59 Ibid.

60 *Connacht Tribune*, 1 Dec. 1920.

61 Joe Togher witness statement, MA, BMH WS 1729.

62 *Galway Observer*, 27 Nov. 1920.

63 *Galway Advertiser*, 8 Feb. 2007.

64 Caroline T. Connolly, 'The *Connacht Tribune*: a history' (unpublished Ma Thesis, UCC, 2003), p. 74.

65 Kostick, *Revolution in Ireland,* p. 147.

66 John D. Costello witness statement, MA, BMH WS 1330.

67 Michael Hynes witness statement, MA, BMH WS 1173.

68 *Connacht Tribune*, 4 Dec. 1920.

69 British Cabinet Meeting, 6 Dec. 1920.

70 Frank Gallagher, *The Anglo-Irish Treaty* (London, 1965), p. 22.

71 Frank Gallagher, *Four glorious years*, (Dublin, 1953), p. 262. This is likely to be incorrect given Hopkinson, Coogan & Ó Fathaigh's positions that it did.

72 Ó Fáthaigh & McMahon, *Recollections of a Galway Gaelic Leaguer*, p. 61.

73 Ibid.

74 *An tÓglach*, 15 Feb. 1921.

75 *Galway Observer*, 26 Feb. 1921.

76 Peter J. McDonnell, 'Action by West Connemara column at Mounterowen' in Gabriel Doherty (ed.), *With the IRA in the fight for Irish freedom* (Cork, 2010), p. 376.

77 Ibid., p. 386.

78 Gilbert Morrissey witness statement, MA, BMH WS 1138.

79 Joe Togher witness statement, MA, BMH WS 674.

80 Michael Hopkinson, *The Irish War of Independence* (Dublin, 2002), p. 138.

81 Lyons, F.S.L., *Ireland since the Famine* (London, 1985), p. 420.

82 *Irish Times*, 17 Mar 1922.

83 Ibid.

84 Michael Brennan witness statement, MA, BMH WS 1068.

85 Brennan, *The war in Clare, 1911–1921*, p. 101.

86 Ó Fathaigh, *Recollections of a Galway Gaelic Leaguer*, p. 84.

87 Gilbert Morrissey witness statement, MA, BMH WS 1138.

88 Tomás Ó Máille, *An tIomaire Rua: cogadh na saoirse i d'tuaisceart Chonamara* (Baila Átha Cliath, 2007), p. 94.

89 Maurice Walsh, *G2: In defence of Ireland: Irish military intelligence, 1918–1945* (Cork, 2010), p. 56.

90 Ó Fathaigh, *Recollections of a Galway Gaelic Leaguer*, p. 50.

91 Joe Togher witness statement, MA, BMH WS 1729.

92 Walsh, *In defence of Ireland*, p. 56.

93 Ó Fáthaigh, *Recollections of a Galway Gaelic Leaguer*, p. 84.

94 Joe Togher witness statement, MA, BMH WS 1729.
95 Walsh, *In defence of Ireland*, p. 56.
96 Ó Fathaigh, *Recollections of a Galway Gaelic Leaguer*, pp 63–7.
97 Fergus Campbell, *The Irish establishment, 1879–1914* (Oxford, 2009), p. 254.
98 Campbell, *Land and revolution*, pp 179–80.
99 John O'Callaghan, *Revolutionary Limerick: the Republican campaign for independence in Limerick: 1913–21* (Dublin, 2010), p. 211. Coleman's book on Longford during the period also shows the need to question Fitzpatrick's dismissive attitude towards local leaders importance, showing as it does that his conclusions are often based on his study of Clare and should not necessarily be applied to the entire country. See Marie Coleman, *County Longford and the Irish revolution* (Dublin, 2003)
1   Michael Hynes witness statement, MA, BMH WS 1173.
2   Joe Togher witness statement, MA, BMH WS 674.

4. THE CIVIL WAR, 1922–3

1   Carlton Younger, *Ireland's Civil War* (London, 1968), p. 304.
2   Walker (ed.), *Parliamentary results in Ireland*, p. 105.
3   *New York Times*, 21 June 1922.
4   Walker (ed.), *Parliamentary results in Ireland,* pp 104–6
5   Ferriter, *Transformation of Ireland*, p. 186.
6   Michael Farry, *The aftermath of revolution: Sligo, 1921–23* (Dublin, 2000), p. 2.
7   Pádraic Óg Ó Ruairc, *The battle for Limerick City* (Cork, 2010), p. 29.
8   Ibid., p. 80.
9   Ibid., p. 65.
10 Michael Hopkinson, *Green against green: the Irish Civil War* (Dublin, 1988), p. 81.
11 Most Revd Dr Fogarty Bishop of Killaloe witness statement, MA, BMH WS 271.

12 Greaves, *Mellows and the Irish Revolution*, p. 291.
13 Eoin Neeson, *The Civil War in Ireland: 1921–23* (Cork, 1966), p. 119.
14 *Irish Times*, 5 July 1922.
15 Ibid.
16 Greaves, *Mellows and the Irish revolution*, p. 330.
17 *Galway Advertiser*, 27 Nov. 2008.
18 *Irish Times*, 27 July 1922.
19 Ibid., 1 June 1922
20 O'Neill, 'Minor famines and relief in County Galway, 1815–1925', p. 472.
21 Kostick, *Revolution in Ireland*, p. 199.
22 Hopkinson, *Green against green*, p. 215.
23 As quoted in *Eleven Galway martyrs* (Galway, 1985), p. 30.
24 Ibid., p. 31.
25 Ibid., p. 38.
26 Ibid.
27 *Tuam Herald*, 29 May 2003.
28 Costello, *The Irish Revolution*, pp 315–17.
29 *New York Times*, 12 Apr. 1923.
30 *Connacht Tribune*, 2 July 1924.
31 Ibid.
32 *Irish Times*, 7 July 2009.
33 O'Neill, *Minor famines and relief in County Galway*, p. 472.
34 *Connacht Tribune*, 6 Sept. 1952.
35 *Galway Advertiser*, 2 Oct. 1975.

CONCLUSION

1   Ferriter, *The transformation of Ireland*, p. 186.
2   Ibid., p. 191.
3   Kevin Connolly, *Easter Rising still holds imagination*. http://news.bbc.co.uk/2/hi/europe/4907566.stm Originally published 16 Apr. 2006. Accessed on 30 May 2010.
4   Patrick Callanan witness statement, MA, BMH WS 405, and Thomas Maguire as quoted in *Eleven Galway martyrs*, p. 30.